# CHANTAL AKERMAN

## PHILOSOPHICAL FILMMAKERS

*Series editor:* Costica Bradatan is Professor of Humanities at Texas Tech University, USA, and Honorary Research Professor of Philosophy at the University of Queensland, Australia. He is the author of *Dying for Ideas: The Dangerous Lives of the Philosophers* (2015), among other books.

Films can ask big questions about human existence: what it means to be alive, to be afraid, to be moral, to be loved. The *Philosophical Filmmakers* series examines the work of influential directors, through the writing of thinkers wanting to grapple with the rocky territory where film and philosophy touch borders.

Each book involves a philosopher engaging with an individual filmmaker's work, revealing how it has inspired the author's own philosophical perspectives and how critical engagement with those films can expand our intellectual horizons.

### Other titles in the series:

*Eric Rohmer*, Vittorio Hösle
*Werner Herzog*, Richard Eldridge
*Terrence Malick*, Robert Sinnerbrink
*Kenneth Lonergan*, Todd May
*Shyam Benegal*, Samir Chopra
*Douglas Sirk*, Robert B. Pippin
*Lucasfilm*, Cyrus R. K. Patell
*Christopher Nolan*, Robbie B. H. Goh

*Alfred Hitchcock*, Mark William Roche
*Luchino Visconti*, Joan Ramon Resina
*Theo Angelopoulos*, Vrasidas Karalis
*Alejandro Jodorowsky*, William Egginton
*István Szabó*, Susan Rubin Suleiman
*Jane Campion*, Bernadette Wegenstein
*David Lean*, Lydia Goehr
Other titles forthcoming:
*Leni Riefenstahl*, Jakob Lothe
*Bong Joon Ho*, Anthony Curtis Adler

# CHANTAL AKERMAN

*Filmmaker and Philosopher*

ANDREJA NOVAKOVIC

BLOOMSBURY ACADEMIC
LONDON • NEW YORK • OXFORD • NEW DELHI • SYDNEY

BLOOMSBURY ACADEMIC

Bloomsbury Publishing Plc

50 Bedford Square, London, WC1B 3DP, UK
1385 Broadway, New York, NY 10018, USA
29 Earlsfort Terrace, Dublin 2, Ireland

BLOOMSBURY, BLOOMSBURY ACADEMIC and the Diana logo are trademarks of Bloomsbury Publishing Plc

First published in Great Britain 2025

Copyright © Andreja Novakovic, 2025

Andreja Novakovic has asserted her right under the Copyright, Designs and Patents Act, 1988, to be identified as Author of this work.

For legal purposes the Acknowledgments on p. vii constitute an extension of this copyright page.

Cover image: The Meetings of Anna (1978)
Collections CINEMATEK - © Fondation Chantal Akerman

All rights reserved. No part of this publication may be reproduced or transmitted in any form or by any means, electronic or mechanical, including photocopying, recording, or any information storage or retrieval system, without prior permission in writing from the publishers.

Bloomsbury Publishing Plc does not have any control over, or responsibility for, any third-party websites referred to or in this book. All internet addresses given in this book were correct at the time of going to press. The author and publisher regret any inconvenience caused if addresses have changed or sites have ceased to exist, but can accept no responsibility for any such changes.

A catalogue record for this book is available from the British Library.

A catalog record for this book is available from the Library of Congress.

ISBN: HB: 978-1-3503-6142-3
PB: 978-1-3503-6141-6
ePDF: 978-1-3503-6143-0
eBook: 978-1-3503-6144-7

Series: Philosophical Filmmakers

Typeset by Deanta Global Publishing Services, Chennai, India
Printed and bound in Great Britain

To find out more about our authors and books visit www.bloomsbury.com and sign up for our newsletters.

*for my mother*

# CONTENTS

*List of Figures* x

Introduction 1
1   Home 23
2   Work 67
3   Love 113
4   Desire 153

*Bibliography* 201
*Index* 207

# FIGURES

1. *La Chambre* directed by Chantal Akerman 1972  14
2. *Hotel Monterey* directed by Chantal Akerman 1972  37
3. *News from Home* directed by Chantal Akerman 1977  41
4. *News from Home* directed by Chantal Akerman 1977  42
5. *D'Est* directed by Chantal Akerman 1993  46
6. *D'Est* directed by Chantal Akerman 1993  48
7. *From the Other Side* directed by Chantal Akerman 2002  50
8. *From the Other Side* directed by Chantal Akerman 2002  52
9. *No Home Movie* directed by Chantal Akerman 2015  54
10. *No Home Movie* directed by Chantal Akerman 2015  57
11. *Blow Up My Town* directed by Chantal Akerman 1968  82
12. *Blow Up My Town* directed by Chantal Akerman 1968  84
13. *Jeanne Dielman 23, quai du Commerce, 1080 Bruxelles* directed by Chantal Akerman 1975  89
14. *Jeanne Dielman 23, quai du Commerce, 1080 Bruxelles* directed by Chantal Akerman 1975  96
15. *Jeanne Dielman 23, quai du Commerce, 1080 Bruxelles* directed by Chantal Akerman 1975  99
16. *Toute une nuit* directed by Chantal Akerman 1982  120
17. *Toute une nuit* directed by Chantal Akerman 1982  121
18. *The Eighties* directed by Chantal Akerman 1983  127
19. *The Eighties* directed by Chantal Akerman 1983  128

20 *Golden Eighties* directed by Chantal Akerman 1986 131
21 *Golden Eighties* directed by Chantal Akerman 1986 135
22 *Je Tu Il Elle* directed by Chantal Akerman 1974 159
23 *Je Tu Il Elle* directed by Chantal Akerman 1974 163
24 *Meetings with Anna* directed by Chantal Akerman 1978 170
25 *La Captive* directed by Chantal Akerman 2000 185
26 *La Captive* directed by Chantal Akerman 2000 189

# Introduction

In a self-portrait called *Chantal Akerman by Chantal Akerman*, Chantal Akerman appears on camera to say that she does not believe in making self-portraits. She wants her films to speak for themselves. After a montage of selected scenes, she reappears for what she describes as her last attempt at a self-portrait: "My name is Chantal Akerman. I was born in Brussels. And that's the truth. It's the truth."[1] As in her films, her desire to capture the truth keeps returning her to her place of origin, to her biography and family history. Akerman was born in 1950 in Brussels to Jewish parents who ran a leather goods store located inside an arcade. Her mother's family had moved to Belgium from a small town in Poland before the war, but they did not manage to escape.[2] Her mother and grandparents were deported to Auschwitz, where her grandparents along with other relatives were killed in 1942. Akerman's mother, Natalia (Nelly) Akerman, a teenager at the time, survived and returned to Brussels, where she married Akerman's father and had two daughters. Akerman made no secret of Nelly's significance for her life and her work. In fact the very first thing Akerman remembers filming was her mother walking into a building and opening the mailbox.[3] Because Nelly never talked about her experiences in the camp, Akerman described her childhood as full of holes.[4] Although her films are haunted by these holes, this could only ever be a part of any portrait of Akerman. In the words of her editor and friend, Claire Atherton, Akerman should also be remembered as "funny and free."[5]

At age fifteen Akerman went to see Godard's *Pierrot Le Fou* at a local movie theater and decided to become a director right then and there. She had discovered the pleasure of watching.[6] In later interviews, Akerman reflected on her choice of medium, mentioning the second commandment against "graven images" (*Bilderverbot*) as an important consideration. How was she going to create images that wouldn't be more "idols in an idolatrous world"?[7] She would thankfully be in good company, for her maternal grandmother, Sidonie Ehrenburg, had painted on large canvases lost during the war. Sidonie had also kept a diary as a teenager that did survive. It opened with the words, "I am a woman! Therefore, I cannot express all my feelings, my thoughts, my sorrows. . . . It is to you my dear diary that I will confide them." Maybe this diary inspired Akerman's own passion for writing and later for incorporating writing into her films. At age eighteen Akerman enrolled in a Belgian film school but dropped out during the first semester to make her first short with a group of classmates.[8] She moved unannounced to New York in 1971 and stayed until 1973. There she met the cinematographer Babette Mangolte, who introduced her to experimental films, most significantly those of Michael Snow. The two of them watched Snow's three-hour-long *La Region Centrale* at the Anthology Film Archives, and as soon as it finished, they stayed to watch it all over again. Akerman eventually moved to Paris, settling into an apartment in the Ménilmontant neighborhood. Even though Paris became her place of residence, she never stopped seeing herself as a nomad. In her words,

"I don't feel I belong anywhere. On the contrary, I have the feeling that I am only attached to the land under my feet. And even there the ground is often a bit shaky."[9]

Akerman is best known for directing *Jeanne Dielman, 23, quai du Commerce, 1080 Bruxelles* (known as *Jeanne Dielman* for short) in 1975, when she was twenty-five years old. It was the film that launched her career, though she never did like that term. In her words, "The day after the screening I was on the map as a filmmaker."[10] When she later reflected on the film's reception, she admitted that she was burdened by the praise it received. "I wondered how to do even better. And I don't know that I have."[11] *Jeanne Dielman*, which covers three days in the life of a Belgian widow, mother, homemaker, and sex worker, is famously a film in which nothing (or almost nothing) happens. *Nothing Happens* is in fact the title of film scholar Ivone Margulies's monograph, a title that captures the impression that *Jeanne Dielman* and other Akerman films tend to make. Akerman was aware of this impression. As she admits, "If I have a reputation for being difficult . . . it is because I love the everyday and want to represent it. In general people go to the movies precisely in order to escape the everyday."[12] But as she also notes, "The flat, the banal, the futile totally shattered me. I had the impression, and I still do, that it is the core of everything."[13] She often depicted ordinary spaces and what happens or does not happen in them, usually filmed at an unhurried pace. In her memoir, *My Mother Laughs*, Akerman refers to everyday happenings as "little nothings." She writes in her mother's voice, "I also love to write what happens even if nothing happens. Yes, there I feel like a person who has something to do, even if nothing happens. But something happens anyway, little nothings."[14]

It was never easy to finance her productions and at least one major project never came to fruition.[15] In the early days, she had to find money in unlikely places: by trading diamond shares on the Antwerp stock exchange and by shortchanging her customers as a cashier at the 55th street Playhouse, a gay porn theater in New York.[16] She even made a short comedy called *Family Business*, in which she is trying to track down a rich uncle in Los Angeles, a fictionalized version of her own struggle to find funding for her films. She regularly hoped that her next film would be a box-office hit, reaching a wider audience, even if just to please her father. Although several of her films garnered critical acclaim, commercial success eluded her until the very end. It is a sad fact that many people probably first heard the name Chantal Akerman when in 2022 *Jeanne Dielman* was selected as the *Sight and Sound* poll's "Best Film of All Time," jumping from thirty-sixth to first place. For a long time, even *Jeanne Dielman* was rarely screened. Jan Decorte, who plays Jeanne Dielman's son in the film, has recently wondered whether this kind of recognition is what the film really needs. He adds that "[i]n any case, she would have laughed heartily at the praise."[17] The good thing is that the poll has spawned new interest in her other films, many of which are still hard to track down. Even if Akerman herself worried that she had peaked at age twenty-five, she went on to make many other masterpieces that deserve to be no less celebrated.

Akerman was restless. She continued to pivot from form to form, from genre to genre. If you compare her early minimalist films with the frenetic flamboyance of her musical, chances are you wouldn't have guessed that they were made by the same person. Then there are her documentaries, ranging from stylized to unpolished, covering topics from the intimate to the global. She seems to have been all over the place. But Akerman is also one of very few women directors who have been labeled "auteurs," an honor usually reserved for men. She invited this image of herself through statements like the following: "I am not making women's films. I'm making Chantal Akerman's films."[18] But Akerman also bore a more complicated relationship to the idea of a singular individual expressing her singular vision than this statement suggests. Many of her films explore the limits that (solitary, lonely) people confront when they undertake projects entirely on their own. She paid close attention to the conditions that hinder or support the pursuit of one's desires, especially when it comes to creative endeavors. Akerman did not ever forget that she relied on a community to get her films made. Mangolte describes the origin of their collaboration: "Chantal and I both had a common goal of making films that would reflect the world in which we lived. We shared a sense of being ignored, and we realized that if we worked together, we could maybe communicate experiences that had not yet been told."[19] The list of her longtime collaborators includes actors Delphine Seyrig and Aurore Clément, her editor Claire Atherton, and her partner, the cellist Sonia Wieder-Atherton (Claire Atherton's sister), all of whom left indelible marks on "Chantal Akerman's films."

When she died in 2015, she left behind a vast output, over forty films in addition to installations and literary texts. Despite her high level of productivity, Akerman often insisted that she spent half her time in bed.[20] She certainly enjoyed depicting herself in bed. For her contribution to the series "Seven Women/ Seven Sins," she chose the sin "sloth," filming herself facing the camera and announcing that "in order to make a film, you have to get up." Or you can just make a film in which you stay mostly in bed. As early as *La Chambre* (1972), the first short she made together with Mangolte while in New York, she is under the covers in the midst of a cluttered apartment. While the camera circles and pans, we catch sight of her in mid-motion, turning her head, chewing an apple, rubbing her eyes. At age thirty-four she experienced her first manic episode, and her energy level permanently plummeted. She used to brim with curiosity. Since then, she says, "I want the days to end early. I go to bed at 5pm, at 8pm, with sleeping pills. Without complaining. That's how it is. I cope with my illness. It's an illness like any other."[21] When Akerman took her own life at sixty-five, her documentary *No Home Movie* had just been released and unfavorably received.[22] The documentary is about her mother's illness and death the previous year, which had left Akerman unsurprisingly adrift. In an interview around that time, Akerman asks, "Now that my mother is no longer here, will I still have something to say?"[23]

Akerman vehemently resisted the ways in which her films were categorized, especially along identity lines. She is credited with making pioneering feminist and lesbian films, and despite the fact that she identified as a feminist and a lesbian, she did not want her films to be included in women's film festivals or gay film festivals. As Kate Rennebohm put it, Akerman "made a career-long habit of rejecting labels."[24] She made an exception only for her Jewish identity, saying, "How would I describe myself? My first response would be, 'I'm a Jewish girl.'"[25] She had several reasons for being suspicious of identity labels. For one, Akerman worried that they would reduce the complexity of her subject matter, turning her characters into tokens of types. For another, Akerman did not want the people who watch her films to use her identity as an excuse to dismiss them as irrelevant to their own lives. Although her work is deeply personal, she did not think that this should distract from its universal aspirations. As she claimed, "I haven't tried to find a compromise between myself and others. I have thought that the more particular I am, the more I address the general."[26] For her, the particular (in principle, *any* particular) can become an opportunity to explore what is general (even what is *most* general). She was once asked during an interview why she made films about such vast and abstract topics like "repetition" and "relation." She answered that "there is nothing else to be attracted to . . . I pour water three times into the glass: that's repetition. I contradict him with the cigarette: that's relation. I'm joking, no? That's life."[27] The film crew was urging her not to smoke inside the building, so to illustrate her point, she broke the rules and lit a cigarette indoors.

\* \* \*

I have come to agree with Akerman that the work should speak for itself—it tends to turn into a self-portrait anyway—but I did want to say a few words about how I found my way to Akerman and why I wrote this book about her. It all started when I was scheduled to teach *Jeanne Dielman* in a philosophy course called "Existentialism in Literature and Film" at the University of California, Berkeley, in the spring of 2021. In preparation for class, I decided to take copious notes so that I could refer back to them instead of having to watch it again before our next meeting. My notes included sentences like the following: "She's in the kitchen wearing a housecoat and heels, the bell rings, so she removes the housecoat and washes her hands, turning off the light, to open the door." As soon as I finished taking them, they struck me as more or less useless. At best, they documented what I happened to notice during this specific viewing, my third time watching it in its entirety. I sympathized with Stanley Cavell, who prefaced his synopsis of *Jeanne Dielman* with the following confession: "I sketch from memory certain events . . . already knowing while little happens that in customary terms would be called interesting, the way it is presented, in its very uneventfulness, makes it almost unthinkable to describe in sufficient detail all it is that you notice."[28]

Maybe Cavell was talking about a general gap between the visual and the verbal, the poverty of description when compared to the richness of perception, which *Jeanne Dielman* throws into especially stark relief. It seems to me that Cavell was also hinting at the way in which *Jeanne Dielman* engrosses attention and keeps it transfixed, leading you to notice more than you otherwise would.[29] Even though the film does not present us with actions and events that many of us have been trained to find entertaining, its three hours and twenty-one minutes can be positively riveting. Thankfully, my students felt the same way. When I asked them to watch it for our class, I braced myself for complaints. We were in the middle of a lockdown, and all courses were being taught on Zoom. Like many instructors, I struggled to "read" the virtual room and often found myself talking to an audience of blank squares with a handful of cameras showing people eating lunch, taking a walk, chatting with roommates. Distraction was at an all-time high. I feared that with *Jeanne Dielman* I was introducing even more tedium into their already uneventful lives. So I was relieved to discover that my students were gripped. They even startled me with their thoughtful reactions to the film, providing me with the first impetus to delve into Akerman.[30] I taught the film again after we returned to the classroom and was again heartened by the enthusiastic response it received.

My own introduction to Akerman also came by way of *Jeanne Dielman*, which I first saw in January 2009. I was a graduate student living in New York and I took the subway with a friend to see a screening of it at the Film Forum on Houston Street. Although this viewing experience is now a blur, images from *Jeanne Dielman*—soaping plates, peeling potatoes, smoothing covers—lingered longer than images from many other films I watched during those years. It later dawned on me that this shouldn't have surprised me. I was writing my dissertation on Hegel's conception of habit. Habit had a relatively bad reputation in Hegel scholarship, where it was often dismissed as an unreflective stage to be surpassed. I was arguing that habit for Hegel is a broad notion that includes intelligent ways of inhabiting one's environment, taking my cue from a statement that Hegel makes in the context of his "Anthropology": "we see that in habit our consciousness is simultaneously present in the subject matter, interested in it, and yet conversely absent from it, indifferent to it."[31] As I read him, Hegel is suggesting that when you are doing what is habitual to you, you needn't be on autopilot. In the case of more complex habits, your awareness is directed at some features of your environment at the expense of others. Although such a directed form of awareness is a positive accomplishment, Hegel does warn that habit is in danger of making you insensitive or inattentive to changing circumstances, even oblivious to what a new situation requires. Hegel refers to this as habit's "deadening" effect.

As a creature of habit, Jeanne Dielman was a perfect fit for my philosophical interests at that time. *Jeanne Dielman* is a film that is like

Hegel alive to both habit's upsides and downsides. Jeanne is absorbed by what she is doing; she is devoting her full attention to the matter at hand; she is inhabiting her world, as small as it may be, seamlessly. But at one mysterious moment, Jeanne grows visibly detached from her routine without knowing how to break out of its pattern, how to forge a different course. She is trapped inside a set of habits that are no longer working for her. As I watched *Jeanne Dielman* on that first afternoon, I was thinking about questions that I had not come across in other contexts. Can a person become so thoroughly habituated that there is nothing left to decide? Is such a life sustainable, livable? Is it even possible to keep going on as before without ever pausing to wonder, why am I doing this, and should I continue? Can such a thoroughly habituated life itself jar a person out of habit's stupor? Or does something have to erupt into such a life from the outside in order to shake a person awake?

Once I started watching other Akerman films, I noticed even deeper affinities with Hegel. One way to summarize Hegel's overall project would be to say that he was the great foe of oppositional thinking.[32] He devised a dialectical method by which he would be able to show that dualisms or binaries turn out to be "differences that are no differences." He does this by setting them into restless motion, thereby repeatedly displaying that neither pole can be neatly distinguished from its opposing other. We see this method in all of his writings, but it is especially vivid in his *Science of Logic* (the "Logic of Essence") where Hegel undertakes to destabilize core philosophical distinctions that are taken to be inescapable—appearance-essence, identity-difference, even reflective-unreflective. For example, Hegel makes the case that essence can only be determined in relation to appearance and vice versa. If there is no recourse to an essence except through an appearance, how could essence be anything other than appearance? And if an appearance is only an appearance in relation to an essence, and so an appearance of an essence, how can appearance be distinguished from essence? If we try to stabilize oppositions by holding one pole in place, Hegel thinks we will find ourselves moving "from nothing to nothing and back again."[33]

It has often been said about Akerman that she distrusted dualisms and binaries, but it would be hasty to think that she simply rejected them.[34] Here are some oppositions that play a prominent role across her films: order and disorder, home and exile, freedom and captivity, and perhaps most prominently, inside and outside. In *My Mother Laughs*, Akerman writes, "I'm going to my apartment in Paris. I have an apartment. It's my home. That's what they say, home. But I don't feel like I have a home or an elsewhere. Somewhere where you feel at home or elsewhere."[35] As this passage indicates, the concept of home has a firm hold on her. Why else describe herself as not being at home? But Akerman is not only denying that she has a home, she is also saying that she does not have a home *or an elsewhere*, thereby challenging the difference between "home" and "elsewhere." When it comes to home and elsewhere, Akerman seems to believe that we cannot completely abandon their distinction, but that we cannot fully accept it. The fact that neither is an option fills her films with tension. They often feature outsiders that are also inside in the sense that they are encircled or enveloped by a context, even when it is not transparent to them, and insiders that are also physically or emotionally outside, no matter how embedded they may appear. Like Hegel in his *Science of Logic*, Akerman's films set such oppositions into restless motion.[36]

So much for the affinities between Akerman and Hegel, whom I won't mention again. As part of a series called "Philosophical Filmmakers," the volume is intended to serve as an encounter between a philosopher (in this case myself) and a filmmaker (Akerman). I have organized it around key themes across her films that have also been of interest to me—home, work, love, and desire—devoting each chapter to a theme and to the films that explore it. Since Akerman made over forty films, I will not attempt to be comprehensive but only to trace a few threads of continuity, with special attention to the films of the 1970s and 1980s, as well as her first and her last. My aim is to bring out Akerman's own process of thinking, which I take to be on display in her films, though these can also be fruitfully supplemented with comments she makes in her interviews. What I hope to highlight is that Akerman is a quintessential "philosophical" filmmaker, by which I mean that she keeps her eye on what is of universal scope, what we might (for lack of a better term) call the human condition. In saying this about her, I do not mean that her films "do philosophy" in the way in which this is often understood, namely, by defending theses, offering counter-examples, or raising objections.[37] On the contrary, Akerman draws a viewer's attention to the human condition not through what she shows on screen, let alone through plot or dialogue, but through how she shows it, specifically through the viewer's own viewing experience of it.

Although she described herself as an autodidact, Akerman even studied philosophy. She tells stories of attending Levinas's lectures in Paris on Saturday mornings that left a lasting impression on her.[38] She was an avid reader who cites figures such as Lacan, Deleuze, Blanchot, Benjamin, Kristeva, and Irigaray in her writings and interviews.[39] In the following, however, I will not explore her debt to the thinkers that she herself mentions. Instead, I want to put Akerman into conversation with a different set of philosophers in the broad sense of that term whose concepts have allowed me to explore home, work, love, and desire in her films because they have helped me draw out Akerman's often original ways of thinking. In these conversations, I mean Akerman to be an active and equal interlocutor. Just to be clear, Akerman's films are not illustrations of ideas to be found elsewhere, especially in philosophical texts. She develops ideas of her own that often depart from and sometimes push against other ways of thinking.

What makes a philosophical approach to her challenging is that her distinct process of thinking is not easy to paraphrase or translate from the visual into the verbal. For Akerman, there is no separation between "form" and "content." She, moreover, did not subscribe to a stark opposition between thinking and feeling. During one interview, she underscores their inseparability through a gesture, moving her hand rapidly from her head to her heart and back again.[40] As she often emphasized, her way of working was intuitive, guided by which shot felt on the nose. She claims that it was because she and Claire Atherton were on the same page that they were able to collaborate for so many years. Akerman also insists that she wanted to evoke feeling. Although she has a reputation for being experimental, hence cerebral, she was never in it for the sheer experiment. When asked to compare her early films to those of other experimental directors whose work was "in the air" at that time, Akerman said, "I think my films are more sentimental."[41] Even though she made *La Chambre* (1972) as homage to Michael Snow's

*Back and Forth*, in which a camera builds suspense by moving back and forth across a classroom, she insisted that *La Chambre* was unlike such a film, not subservient to a concept or an idea. As you watch *La Chambre*, "you have the feeling of a room, a young woman, of New York, something."[42] (Figure 1)

Akerman was suspicious of big feelings. She claimed that American directors such as Hitchcock, whom she greatly admired, "don't allow the viewer to be free before the film. That's what makes a good director and I do the opposite . . . And I hope that the viewer feels free to feel the film and not just understand it."[43] She wanted to "free" feeling, rather than prompting a specific emotional response. What does a person feel when they feel a film? Is it just a matter of giving feelings, whichever happen to arise, free rein? As Akerman specifies, to be free to feel a film is to feel its duration. What she is rendering

FIGURE 1 La Chambre *directed by Chantal Akerman 1972. Collections CINEMATEK—© Fondation Chantal Akerman.*

is the passage of time. She made this point gleefully every chance she got, for example in the following:

> When people are enjoying a film they say "I didn't see the time go by"... but I think that when time flies and you don't see time passing by you are robbed of an hour and a half or two hours of your life. Because all you have in life is time... With my films you're aware of every second passing through your body.[44]

She admits that this is not a pleasant feeling, a feeling we welcome. She even proposes that it is to confront time's rush toward the ultimate end.[45] It is to be made aware that every moment you are occupied watching her film is a moment that has irreversibly vanished. But Akerman is not trying to rob you of your time. Instead, she takes herself to be honoring the time you have left. For her, experiencing time's passage is a way of expanding it, allowing every second to pass through your body. What fascinates her about duration is that it is both intensely personal and widely shared.

The chapters in this volume are only loosely connected not as steps in an argument but as stages in Akerman's evolving interests. That said, they are unified by Akerman's longstanding preoccupation with filming inner life. She is interested in strategies for showing inner life as genuinely inner on screen, so as invisible or illegible, or not readily visible or legible to an audience. When it comes to the question of interiority, approaches to Akerman tend to diverge. Some conclude that Akerman is not interested in the interiority of her characters or that she is presenting them as lacking interiority, either because they say very little or because what they say does not give a lot away.

Others conclude that she shows her characters as suffering from pathologies such as depression, obsessive-compulsion, and so on. I think both are off the mark. What Akerman is after is what Marcel Proust calls "that unknowable thing" when he writes: "by exploring a small part of the great empty zone that spread around me, I had succeeded only in pushing further back into that unknowable thing—when we actually try to picture it for ourselves—the real life of another human being."[46] The real life of another human includes the thoughts and feelings they do not divulge or disclose, as well as the habits they enact when no one is watching. The key contrast is not between a mind (inner) and a body (outer), but between what someone presents to others and what they prefer to keep to themselves.

Akerman's own focus on spheres of privacy is inspired by her mother, a woman who laughed a lot and loved to chat but withheld her traumatic experiences from her daughter. If Akerman's films are all about her mother even when they do not appear to be, it is because they grapple with "this unknowable thing" to which her mother drew her attention. Nelly's refusal to share might have been a source of personal frustration, but in her work, Akerman turns it into a positive vision. How do you preserve a person's interiority while filming them? And how can you even enjoy watching them when so much remains obscured or concealed? Akerman develops a style of filmmaking that is attentive but non-intrusive. She consistently maintains a respectful distance from her figures on screen, whether they are real people or fictional characters, allowing them to remain partly mysterious. Maintaining a respectful distance is a way of respecting privacy, letting them show whatever it is that they want to show, rather than trying to spy on their real lives or probe their inner depths. Although Akerman's work is decidedly not didactic, it sometimes suggests that this might be a better mode of engagement.

In any case, Akerman turns this almost ethical imperative into a source of aesthetic pleasure. She demonstrates that it can be enticing, even satisfying, to linger on the surfaces of things, like the gleaming veneers that pervade Jeanne Dielman's apartment on *rue du Commerce* and reflect the light that reaches them. It is all the more enticing and satisfying when you suspect that there would have been more to discover behind or beneath, but you also realize that you never will, in part because Akerman has chosen not to go there. We can think of this as a matter of lingering on the surfaces of the people on screen, on their external appearance. What makes their appearances pleasurable would be Akerman's intimation of something that does not meet our eye, at least not directly. But we can also think of it as a matter of lingering on the surface of her films, on what Susan Sontag described as the "pure, untranslatable, sensuous immediacy" of the filmed image.[47] It is the sheer look of them that makes Akerman's films often so affecting, even long after.

As a final note, it is important not to exaggerate the borders around privacy, as if the divide between inner and outer lives, or between private and public lives, were stable and fixed. In Akerman's films, gestures and movements sometimes express more than is intended, and certainly more than is said. But Akerman also turns her focus upon her own inner life when she explores "the great empty zone that spreads around *her*" (to return to Proust's words). Even when her films do not include information from her biography or family history, they feature the mixture of thoughts and feelings that happened to enter her mind during their making. This does not render her films insulated and inaccessible, as if she were absorbed by something no one else could possibly understand. Instead, Akerman's approach erodes any sharp boundary between her own interiority and that of her viewer. As Emily LaBarge has recently written, Akerman's films are "offerings without arguments."[48] What they offer is an invitation not only to surrender to their duration but also to relate to them in a personal way by contributing whatever thoughts and feelings enter your mind while watching. In the following chapters, I tried my best to take this to heart.

I am grateful to Dicky Bahto, Aglaya Glebova, Patrick Londen, Fred Neuhouser, Karen Ng, and Lauren Rosenblum for their feedback, and to Judith Butler for passing this project on to me. Thank you to the participants of the conference on *Alltäglichkeit* at the Free University of Berlin and of Phil Forum at UC Berkeley, where I presented versions of the second chapter. Thank you also to Katie Coyne for preparing the index. I am indebted to the Chantal Akerman Foundation for access to *Toute une nuit* and for the stills included here, to the podcast *The Akerman Year* by Kate Rennebohm and Simon Howell for pointing me in many fruitful directions, to Costica Bradatan for his editorial guidance, and to an anonymous referee for helpful suggestions. Very special thanks are due to Francey Russell for inspiring me to start writing about film and to Amanda Lopatin for talking to me about all things Akerman and for inspiring me to think more deeply and creatively about her films. I am most grateful to Rolf Horstmann for suggesting I write this book, for encouraging me during the process, and for now making it difficult to imagine a better way to spend one's time than watching and rewatching Akerman's films. It is only fitting that the book be dedicated to my mother, Lidija Novakovic, for her immeasurable influence and support.

## Notes

1 *Chantal Akerman by Chantal Akerman.*
2 See Tine Rahel Völcker, *Chantal Akermans Verschwinden*. This is a book that traces Akerman's Polish roots.
3 Godard interview: https://derives.tv/jean-luc-godard-chantal-akerman/.
4 She refers to her story as "full of holes" in *Chantal Akerman: Autoportrait en Cinéaste*, p. 30.
5 http://www.sensesofcinema.com/2015/chantal-akerman/chantal-akerman-claire-atherton/.
6 See Sandy Flitterman-Lewis, *To Desire Differently*, pp. 20 and 307. She translates "*la jouissance du voir*" as "the erotics of vision" and "the ecstasy of seeing."
7 Pajama Interview: http://www.lolajournal.com/2/pajama.html. See also the interview with Godard, where she discusses her desire to transgress this commandment.
8 Institut National Supérieur des Arts du Spectacle et des Techniques de Diffusion.
9 Marion Schmid, *Chantal Akerman*, p. 12 (Schmid's translation of the original French).
10 Criterion Channel interview.
11 Criterion Channel interview.
12 Quoted in Jonathan Rosenbaum, "Place and Displacement."
13 Akerman, *Autoportrait*, p. 49–52: "Le plat, le banal, le sens effet, me bouleversaient totalement. J'avais l'impression, et je l'ai toujours, que c'est là que tout se trouve."

14  Akerman, *My Mother Laughs*, p. 21.

15  The project was supposed to be based on "The Manor" by Isaac Bashevis Singer.

16  Interview with Gary Indiana: https://www.artforum.com/print/198306/getting-ready-for-the-golden-eighties-a-conversation-with-chantal-akerman-35484.

17  From *Chantal Akerman, Travelling*, p. 28.

18  Quoted in Margulies, *Nothing Happens*, p. 12.

19  Babette Mangolte, *Selected Writings*, pp. 357–8.

20  Pajama Interview.

21  Ibid.

22  Kate Zambreno: "[Chantal Akerman] had committed suicide. Some believe she was in despair over her last film being booed at a festival, a film that takes place almost entirely in her elderly mother's Brussels apartment before her mother's death, a film Akerman edited while still deep in grief" (*Drifts*, p. 80). According to Mangolte, Akerman sometimes decided to stop taking her medication while she was working on a project (*Selected Writings*, p. 364).

23  *I Don't Belong Anywhere: The Cinema of Chantal Akerman*, documentary by Marianne Lambert.

24  Kate Rennebohm, "La Ressasseuse," p. 7.

25  Pajama Interview: "But if you asked me, 'what does it mean to be Jewish?' I wouldn't be able to tell you." As her career progressed, she started making films with increasingly explicit Jewish themes. An example would be *American Stories: Food, Family, Philosophy*, which is about Jewish immigrants in New York and which she allowed to be screened at Jewish film festivals.

26  Quoted in Patricia White, "*Camera Obscura* and Chantal Akerman," p. 2.

27  *Chantal Akerman, From Here*.

28  Cavell, *Here and There: Sites of Philosophy*, p. 58. This statement also appears in "The World as Things," p. 255.

29  Salomé Aguilera Skvirsky writes, "we become absorbed by Jeanne's absorption," for her satisfaction in performing her daily chores becomes our

satisfaction in watching her do it (*Process Genre*, p. 206). See also Skvirsky, pp. 202–3, and Margulies, *Nothing Happens*, p. ix.

30  Many who teach this film have noted student enthusiasm. See, for example, Patricia White: http://www.thecine-files.com/teaching-jeanne-dielman-23-quai-du-commerce-1080-bruxelles/.

31  Hegel, *Encyclopedia III*, §410A, my translation.

32  I am borrowing this expression from Sellars, who famously called Hegel "the great foe of immediacy."

33  This is to describe Hegel's movement of reflection in "subjective" terms, in terms of the movement that the reader is enacting and undergoing, which is potentially misleading.

34  See Marion Schmid, *Chantal Akerman*, p. 2.

35  Ibid., p. 5.

36  The comparison might seem farfetched, but some critics have used "dialectical" to describe her approach. See Steven Jacobs, "Semiotics of the Living Room," who talks about her "dialectics between interior and exterior spaces." In the Pajama Interview, Akerman herself rejects the term "dialectics" for being too closely associated with Marx. This does necessarily implicate Hegel, whom she does not mention.

37  There is an ongoing debate in the philosophy of film as to whether films "can philosophize," which is a formulation that comes from Stephen Mulhall's *On Film*.

38  Pajama Interview. She claims that after her first manic episode, she forgot the content of these lectures.

39  She mentions some of them in *Autoportrait En Cinéaste* and in various interviews.

40  *I Don't Belong Anywhere: The Cinema of Chantal Akerman*.

41  https://www.artforum.com/print/198306/getting-ready-for-the-golden-eighties-a-conversation-with-chantal-akerman-35484.

42  *Chantal Akerman: From Here*.

43  *I Don't Belong Anywhere: The Cinema of Chantal Akerman*.

44 https://www.sensesofcinema.com/2015/chantal-akerman/vivian-ostrovsky-tribute/.
45 *Chantal Akerman, From Here.*
46 Marcel Proust, *The Prisoner*, p. 52.
47 Susan Sontag, *Against Interpretation: And Other Essays.*
48 https://yalereview.org/article/emily-labarge-chantal-akerman.

# 1

# Home

## World Travel

Akerman's documentaries travel the world. From her early *Hotel Monterey* (1972) to her final *No Home Movie* (2015), they traverse a vast stretch of geography: New York, Belgium, Eastern Europe, Tel Aviv, a small town in Texas, the US-Mexico border. Since Akerman often described herself as a nomad who does not belong anywhere, her camera imitates her own tendency to keep wandering, featuring people who are similarly on the go, loitering on street corners, in train stations or hotel lobbies, as well as people enclosed or entrapped in buildings or rooms. By venturing to remote places, Akerman's documentaries also investigate the flipside of travel—what it is to be at home somewhere. She arrives at the concept of home negatively via what it is not to be at home. The term "home" is often used as a synonym for a private space, but it can also be used to refer to a larger context in which you know your way around. Many of Akerman's films are indeed set in domestic interiors, thereby invoking a contrast between home and outside. But her documentaries, in particular, explore "home" in an expanded sense as a distinct way of inhabiting one's environment even when one happens to be on the subway or in an elevator. To be at home would be to be in a world that is readily intelligible to you and that you are able to navigate competently and confidently. To be at home in the world in this sense would be to feel at home, though it wouldn't be reducible to a feeling. For one, some worlds or parts of the world are hostile or inhospitable, so whether you feel at home could say something about the context in which you find yourself. For another, whether a person is at home can be observed and hence documented. Someone at home would look uninhibited and unhindered, whereas someone not at home would be lacking this visible ease, appearing hesitant, clumsy, disoriented, or distracted.

Akerman's documentaries across her career—specifically *Hotel Monterey*, *News from Home*, *D'Est*, *From the Other Side*, and *No Home Movie*—address this concept of home in one way or another, the term even appearing in two of these titles.[1] When I speak about her documentaries, I do not have in mind a specific genre. Instead, I mean her non-fiction films that cover a wide stylistic range. In these films, we witness Akerman grappling with her complicated feelings around the concept of home. Akerman often emphasized that her self-conception as someone who never stops wandering is for her connected to her Jewish identity and to the myth of the "Wandering Jew."[2] Although she did not find it easy to never feel at home, her films are also suspicious of the temptation to chase this feeling. It is part of her effort to set oppositions into motion, in this case, the opposition between the view from within and the view from without. One side would be the "absorbed insider" who inhabits their context seamlessly, the other side the "detached outsider" looking into a world to which they do not belong. What Akerman does is to reveal continuity between these two perspectives: just as the outsider cannot fully detach, so the insider cannot fully avoid detaching. In this way, her documentaries invite the question of whether being at home is a stable condition for anyone, and relatedly, whether it is an ideal worth pursuing.

This is not meant to erase the very real difference between insider and outsider in the political sense, a difference rooted in histories of exclusion, displacement, and destruction. In fact, it is these histories that draw Akerman to specific places, for in them she recognizes reverberations of her own. Although Akerman's documentaries are in many cases political in their subject matter, this has more to do with the experience she is capturing than with the position she is taking. She makes clear that she is less interested in large-scale political events and actions than she is in everyday examples of resistance. As she puts it, "I love the little things: one can resist in a thousand ways."[3] She also once said, "In my films I follow an opposite trajectory to that of the makers of political films. They have a skeleton, an idea and then they put on flesh: I have in the first place the flesh, the skeleton appears later."[4] As a metaphor, this statement pertains to her process of moving from the concrete image to the abstract concept, rather than the other way. But her statement can also be taken less metaphorically as making embodiment undeniable.[5] Bodies are obviously treated very differently, and some people are more at ease in their skin than others. But her documentaries are sensitive to the fact that each perspective at play in them—the one filming, being filmed, and viewing the film—is encumbered by a body and its point of view. Here, Akerman is not only documenting particular regions of the world and their inhabitants, although she is doing that as well;

these are films more generally about what it is like to live inside a human body.

Akerman's documentaries explore the concept of home along two lines. On one level, they make being at home their theme by showing an array of people in motion and the spaces they leave behind. Empty rooms were once occupied by those no longer present and even those we now see are not here to stay. Her attention to what vanishes and what remains suggests a deeper point, only ever intimated by what we are shown: that even for those who manage to carve out a home, it is in the best-case scenario a temporary abode built on unstable ground. This suggests one respect in which even her documentaries are all about her mother. They do not allow us to forget the fact of mortality, which weighed especially heavily in her mother's case. On another level, her documentaries are also exploring the nature of perceptual experience and drawing attention to it through the experience of watching her films.[6] In them, she develops a self-aware approach to documenting. These documentaries are not journalistic or ethnographic because they repeatedly foreground that which mediates her access to what is present.[7] Although Akerman documents with genuine curiosity, her gaze is never carefree, for whatever she perceives in the moment, she perceives as shaped by the past. She is thereby challenging whether it is possible and whether it is desirable to rid oneself of one's burdens. Akerman is uniquely attuned to the weight she carries wherever she goes. In these documentaries, she often inserts traces of herself and places her camera at her own low eye level, lest we confuse it with the view of a bird or a god.

In this way, Akerman's documentaries raise questions about the relationship of non-fiction films to the reality that they ostensibly represent. Akerman titled a documentary-based installation "Bordering on Fiction," and she elsewhere said that she did not believe that there is "such a wall between the two genres."[8] She also claimed that making documentaries allowed her to be more imaginative and creative because shooting them was possible with a small crew and editing them was not constrained by a narrative sequence. Since her non-fictional films are often self-conscious, they also raise questions about the way in which she is representing herself in them.[9] Are we seeing the real Akerman, or is her presented "self" also bordering on fiction? According to Stanley Cavell, documentary filmmakers are especially tempted to make their own presence known by filming the camera, "as if to justify [their] intrusion upon [their] subject."[10] He considers these tactics to be facile. Who isn't already aware that they are viewing a filmed object? Cavell goes on:

> But this guilty impulse, produced, it may be, by the film-maker's denial of the only thing that matters; that the subject be allowed to reveal itself. The denial may be in spirit or in fact, an unwillingness to see what is revealed or an inability to wait for its revelation ... Your position is no more localizable beforehand that the knowledge itself is.[11]

His worry is that self-awareness risks centering oneself at the expense of one's subject matter. Also, by locating your own position in advance, you are potentially limiting what you are willing to discover.

Akerman affirms this sentiment to a degree. She claims, "For a documentary, I become an empty sponge: if you start off with a preconceived idea, you'll obtain it—but you won't see a thing."[12] While documentary filmmaking calls for maximal open-mindedness, her practice also denies that by bringing yourself into the picture, you are drawing attention away from others. As Akerman puts it, "When you try to show reality in cinema, most of the time it is totally false. But when you show what's going on in people's minds that's very cinematic."[13] This has led to the impression that she is representing the states of her own consciousness, what is going on in her mind while she is making the film.[14] Her documentaries can indeed be described as "moody" films, usually pervaded by dark moods such as loneliness or mourning, though they also include moments of levity. But calling them states of her own consciousness fuels the fantasy that non-fiction films should aspire to represent reality immediately or neutrally, an instance of what Cavell describes as the fantasy of the world unseen.

I do not think that this is a fantasy that Akerman shares. Like all of Akerman's films, her documentary filmmaking is informed by the conviction that the burdens she brings to bear to what she sees are not obstacles to seeing what is there. In fact, these burdens allow her to perceive more, or more clearly. This is not to assume that all burdens are equally illuminating. In Akerman's case, it seems to be the fact that she does not feel at home anywhere that makes her attuned to, and that draws her camera to, a similar quality outside herself. Her unabashed form of self-reflection turns out to be in the service of discovering the real lives of other people by showing that this experience of not being at home anywhere is more common than we might have noticed.

## In Between Worlds

I described Akerman's documentaries as traveling the world, but they also call to mind "world"-travel, by which I mean traveling to "worlds" by interacting with the people who live there and learning to perceive these "worlds" from an internal point of view. "World"-travel would then be different from simply traversing a stretch of geography in order to arrive at a different location in space. In fact, "world"-travel might not even require going elsewhere—you could in principle do it by staying put. "World"-travel in this sense emerges out of Latina feminist philosophy. It is a term coined by Maria Lugones and a concept that features also in the writings of Gloria Anzaldúa and Mariana Ortega. "World"-travel can be identified with the perspective of those who, like Akerman, are never fully at home anywhere. As Lugones puts it, "When I think of my own people, the only people I can think of as my own are transitionals, liminals, border-dwellers, 'world'-travelers, beings in the middle of either/or."[15] Akerman shares an affinity with such beings in the middle. But we can also say that when seen through Akerman's lens, everyone starts to look a little like a being in the middle. Even when someone is not moving among actual worlds, they strike her as being in a state of limbo, "poised between birth and death."[16] In the end, anyone Akerman films is revealed to be a visitor, just passing through.

One way to arrive at an understanding of "world"-travel would be to contrast it with the notion of being at home in the world. Martin Heidegger is arguably the philosopher of the concept of home in this expanded sense.[17] In *Being and Time*, being at home—or "being-in-the-world" (*in-der-Welt-sein*)—is integral to his analysis of what it is to be a human being (*Dasein*). To be a human being is to be "worldly," in-the-world. Heidegger rejects two ways of interpreting this claim. He does not mean that the human being is an object dropped into the world like a coin into a wallet. He also does not mean that a human being relates to the world as an object or as a collection of objects. As it is sometimes expressed, for Heidegger the human being is "always already" in the world, embedded in a context comprised of tools that are ready-to-hand. This means that human beings relate to the world as a meaningful context, and that human beings inhabit this context for the most part unreflectively, except when a problem arises, for instance, a hammer breaks down. But it is clear that for Heidegger these are exceptional circumstances. So Heidegger is starting from the positive case, from being at home in the world, rather than from the negative case, from things in your world going awry.

There are many reasons that speak against bringing Heidegger into a book about Akerman. His antisemitism and affiliation with National Socialism are well known. But there is one aspect of Heidegger's notion of being-in-the-world that is useful for clarifying Akerman's approach in her documentaries. Heidegger's conception of "moods" can help us see why it would be a mistake to assume that Akerman is either documenting reality or documenting her own consciousness. For one, Heidegger holds that moods permeate our being-in-the-world even when we do not notice them. We are always in some mood or other. For another, Heidegger claims that a mood "comes neither from 'outside' nor from 'inside,' but arises out of being-in-the-world."[18] Just like meaning is not projected onto an otherwise meaningless world, so moods do not "color" an otherwise mood-less world.[19] Instead, moods open up the world, disclosing it as the meaningful context that it is. Heidegger is especially interested in the mood of anxiety, which he thinks has the power to reveal that the human being is always also "home-less" [*unheimlich*]. Despite his focus on what it is to be at home in the world, it would be fair to say that Heidegger is likewise challenging an understanding of home that sits uncomfortably with what he calls our "being-towards-death."

You might nevertheless worry that Heidegger's description of being at home in the world is too narrow, or that it privileges certain experiences over others. In *In Between*, Mariana Ortega argues that Heidegger is illegitimately generalizing from his own case of being for the most part comfortable in his own world. In her words, "multiplicitous selves in the margins are constantly experiencing disruptions in their everyday being-in-worlds or instances of what I describe as not-being-at-ease. It points to a problem in Heidegger's discussion—namely, that Heidegger's existential analytic does not fully capture the lived experience of marginalized selves highlighted by Latina feminists."[20] Although Ortega thinks that Heidegger is right to say that we are always already in the world, *the* world for marginalized people is composed of multiple "worlds" that overlap in complicated and challenging ways.[21] This means that their practical orientation is regularly disrupted.[22] It might be the case that everyone is occasionally not at ease in their own skin, but for marginalized people, not being at ease is a constant feature of their everyday lives. According to Ortega, Heidegger's description of being-in-the-world cannot be extended to the experiences of those who find themselves in liminal spaces, unable to relax wherever they happen to be.

Ortega is taking inspiration from Gloria Anzaldúa's *Borderlands/La Frontera*, in which Anzaldúa describes her experience of inhabiting a "borderland," "a vague and undetermined place created by the emotional residue of an unnatural boundary."[23] For Anzaldúa, there is the literal borderland in which she grew up, the Rio Grande Valley in the south of Texas, an area that once belonged to Mexico and was seized by the United States; then there is the emotional borderland that tracks the psychic impact of any artificial line demarcating inside and outside.[24] Ortega is suggesting that we arrive at a very different picture of being-in-the-world as such if we take the experience in the borderland as our point of departure. In her view, what we discover is that to be a human being is to be a "multiplicitous self" that is both in-worlds and in between worlds. Ortega is using the term "multiplicitous self" to pick out marginalized selves, as well as to designate the structure of selfhood as such. Although being in worlds and between worlds applies also to those in the center, we shouldn't be surprised that it tends to get noticed more readily by those in the margin. Ortega goes on to develop an alternative conception of home as a sense of imperfect and incomplete belonging.[25] She thinks that this alternative conception prevents us from idealizing homes as havens where we were once our true selves while preventing us from reducing homes to places of violence.[26]

Ortega is also influenced by Maria Lugones, who puts forward a concept of a "world" that bears some resemblance to Heidegger's being-in-the-world. World is a term Lugones places in quotation marks because she wants to indicate that she means actual worlds inhabited by flesh-and-blood people, rather than merely possible worlds or utopian worlds.[27] In her "Playfulness, 'World'-Travel, and Loving Perception," Lugones develops this notion of "world" by reflecting on her own experience of "world"-travel, a practice she recommends as "a skillful, creative, rich, enriching and, given certain circumstances, as a loving way of being and living."[28] "World"-travel is an "acquired flexibility in shifting from the mainstream construction of life where [the outsider] is constructed as an outsider to other constructions of life where she is more or less 'at home'. This flexibility is necessary for the outsider but it can also be willfully exercised by the outsider or by those who are at ease in the mainstream."[29] To "world"-travel is to move between two poles: the "mainstream" construction that positions the outsider as an outsider, and the construction according to which the outsider is more or less at home—more or less, never perfectly. This makes "world"-travel a shift in perspective that requires engaging with the people who live in a "world" and learning to see their "world" lovingly; in short, to see it as they do. Some people are compelled to "world"-travel by their circumstances, though Lugones allows that others learn it through effort.[30] "World"-travel for her is a political practice of resistance and liberation that forges coalitions across identity lines.[31]

What her concept of "world" brings to the fore is that we can find ourselves in the same location in space but live in different "worlds" in her sense. Lugones provides a telling example of how she learned to "world"-travel that will resonate with Akerman's own documentary practice, to which I am about to turn.[32] Even though Lugones was living in close proximity to her mother, and even though she was convinced that she loved her mother, Lugones came to realize that she had failed to travel to her mother's "world." As she admits,

> Loving my mother also required that I see with her eyes, that I go into my mother's "world," that I see both of us as we are constructed in her "world," that I witness her own sense of herself from within her "world". . . . Only then could I see her as a subject, even if one

subjected, and only then could I see at all how meaning could arise fully between us.³³

As a child, Lugones identified with her mother by taking her for granted and by treating her as an extension of herself. But she came to realize that to love is to love across difference, hence across a divide between herself and her mother that first needed to be wedged.

Mothers appear regularly in the writings of philosophers, as they do in Akerman's films. Even philosophical texts can turn to the personal in order to illuminate a general point. For example, Anzaldúa picks up a similar question that Lugones raises about what is required to love at all, including one's own mother, when she reflects on what it took for her to separate from her mother and her mother's "world." As Anzaldúa puts it, "To this day I'm not sure where I found the strength to leave the source, the mother, disengage from my family, *mi tierra, mi gente,* and all that picture stood for. I had to leave home so I could find myself, find my own intrinsic nature buried under the personality that had been imposed on me."³⁴ Anzaldúa argues that this departure, which began in her childhood when she started talking back to her mother, enabled her to discover herself as an individual, and as a lesbian to whom her culture of origin was inhospitable. This prevents Anzaldúa from romanticizing the home she left behind. Akerman herself will approach the question of identity somewhat differently, since she would not have accepted the idea of an intrinsic nature. But Akerman probably would have agreed with Anzaldúa that it is far more difficult to become oneself if one remains in a mother's immediate orbit. Maybe it is the case that traveling back to a "world," including one's mother's "world," can only happen in the wake of leaving it irretrievably behind. In any case, it is a prospect with which Akerman was confronted.

## Lonely City

In the early 1970s, Akerman was in her early twenties living in New York. She had left on the spur of the moment without telling anyone. It was her first time away from her home, from Brussels, from her mother. She felt like a vagabond without a permanent address. During the two years she lived in the city, she grew as a filmmaker at an exponential rate, discovering structural films and tailoring this style to her own vision. "Structural film," a term coined by P. Adams Sitney, follows a predetermined structure, privileges form over content, and draws attention to the film's medium.[35] One way in which these films drew attention to the medium is by mechanizing or automating the filming process, making it seem as if the lens is detached from any person who could give it direction. Although Akerman sometimes plays with this trope, especially through her tracking shots, it is also clear that her lens is very much attached to her own person.[36] Her early experimental documentaries are not yet "world"-traveling films, since they do not bring their subjects to flesh-and-blood life. But there is another notion from Lugones that might be more apt: "streetwalking," adopting an observational perspective that is not detached from what it documents but remains decidedly street-level.[37]

Akerman made two documentaries in a broadly structural style that reflect on this period of her life in New York, both made in collaboration with Babette Mangolte. The first is her silent documentary *Hotel Monterey* from 1972. In hindsight, she says of its making: "I can breathe, I'm really a filmmaker."[38] The second, *News from Home*, was made in 1976 after she had already moved away from New York.[39] Often described as an essay film, it includes observational footage. What binds the two films together is that they show an emotionally inflected image of New York. This makes them both personal and impersonal, about her experience of the city and about the city itself. They are also self-conscious films insofar as they refer to Akerman's role in their making, employing two strategies for doing so, neither of which is as facile as simply filming the camera. One strategy is to show the world from Akerman's visual vantage point, allegedly five feet one. As Akerman often emphasized, seeing things from relatively close to the ground is just showing the world as it looks to her.[40] Another strategy is to feature people noticing that they are being filmed by her, sometimes responding by retreating.[41] Whether or not she is noticed is a question of chance; it is not something that she can predict or control. But it is revealing of the city and of her experience living in it how rarely she is.

*Hotel Monterey* was shot inside a welfare hotel for people without a permanent address, a space for transients in a very literal sense. Akerman's choice of location tells us a lot about what she was paying attention to—she is struck by those cast out of a stable social fabric. According to Mangolte, Akerman lived at this hotel for several weeks upon her arrival.[42] If we already know that Akerman was feeling like a vagabond at that time, we won't be surprised that she was drawn to vagabonds. But we are not told any facts from Akerman's life in the film, which is without a soundtrack. It is often described as "structural" because it subscribes to formal constraints, though Akerman stressed that she had less of a plan for it than would have been typical. Her only constraint is that she was committed from the start to shooting in one day and moving from the main floor to the top, but she relied on her feeling while filming in choosing her subjects. The film appears to be merely observing what is happening, though there is a feeling of drifting that is hard to locate. In its concluding shot, we arrive on the roof of the hotel to find a bright sky, the Hudson River, early morning traffic, probably relieved to exit this confined space and to remember that the hotel is not a world onto itself. It exists in a larger context, the city of New York.[43]

*Hotel Monterey* opens with a scene in the lobby, though the setting is not immediately apparent. What we see is a small mirror on a wall reflecting the image of two people talking (Figure 2). We are being primed to expect that our access is going to be indirect. These people will remain at a distance, even when they approach the camera or the

FIGURE 2 Hotel Monterey *directed by Chantal Akerman 1972. Collections CINEMATEK—© Fondation Chantal Akerman.*

camera approaches them. But Akerman is also intentionally looking away from their lives. With the exception of a few tracking shots, her camera hardly moves and never follows anyone down the hall and into their rooms. It is a way of respecting people's privacy or a way of honoring the difficulty of their situation. We are shown a few people inside their rooms with their backs turned, as well as shots of rooms with clutter left behind. What she is emphasizing is that these are people who do not live here. Hotel Monterey has seen many guests pass through its lobby.[44] In the film, its current occupants turn into fleeting presences on the screen. While the camera is positioned outside the elevator facing its doors, the people we see entering and exiting have distinct faces; we can tell them for the most part apart. But once the camera enters the elevator and watches its gliding doors from within, the people crowded inside turn into dark shadows, indistinguishable silhouettes. What could be more liminal than an elevator and the close physical proximity it affords, over in less than a minute?

*Hotel Monterey* also features a couple of memorable individuals. A man in a bowtie is sitting in an armchair next to an unmade bed, everything immobile except for his darting eyes. A pregnant woman is glimpsed through a door frame, basked in a light whose source we do not see.[45] Kate Zambreno compares her to a painting by Vermeer.[46] In fact, stills from Akerman's films have often been compared to paintings, for instance Edward Hopper's. These early films are arguably more obviously influenced by minimalist art known for exaggerating or replicating forms and patterns, an influence especially vivid in *Hotel Monterey*.[47] In a later shot, the camera moves up and down an empty hallway, seemingly as stir-crazy as the viewer. Akerman alludes to minimalist art when she describes her aims as follows: "When you look at a picture, if you look just one second you get the information, 'that's a corridor.' But after a while you forget it's a corridor, you just see that it's yellow, red, lines: and then it comes back as a corridor."[48] In the film, she explores an oscillation between perceiving the hotel and its inhabitants and abstracting from them, turning them into forms and patterns. It is central to the film that she is hitting both registers at once. How long can you observe people before you start seeing them as ghostly shapes? And how long before your attention shifts to the endlessly repetitive opening and closing of the elevator doors?

*News from Home*, made four years later, consists of long shots of New York superimposed by a soundtrack of Akerman reading aloud letters, the titular letters from "home."[49] Although the footage was shot during Akerman's visit to the city in 1976, she received these letters from her mother a few years earlier. The letters are about her mother's everyday concerns back in Brussels, primarily about relatives, the states of their health and the states of their marriages. The mother also pleads with her daughter to write more often and to describe her life in New York in more detail—where is she living, how is she getting by? Akerman's replies, not included in the film, are insufficient to satisfy her mother. While we hear the mother's letters at growing intervals, we are shown images of people sitting on chairs or walking through doors, kids playing with a fire hydrant or playing baseball, bustling intersections and crowded subway cars. These are all shot from her vantage point, reflecting the perspective of New York that would have been available to Akerman.[50] The conjunction of letters and images produces a strong impression of Akerman stuck between two worlds, pulled in two directions, home and away from home. The urban footage locates her uneasy homesickness in a time and place, but it also stands in tension with the letters, showing a world far from Brussels, a world to which her past is irrelevant.[51] The people she films do not know or care about Akerman's life. There is even a growing competition between the sounds of New York and Akerman's voice. More and more frequently, the city drowns out the news from home.

While *News from Home* proliferates self-reflection, the self at its center is only thinly drawn. Most prominently, there is Akerman's acoustic presence, making it clear that this is not a straightforward documentary about New York, but a film that is better described in terms of her relationship to the city, a relationship shaped by her enduring connection to her family. Despite the fact that we hear her, it would be too quick to conclude that Akerman is inserting herself as an individual into this film. In fact, Akerman's individuality is a question raised by the very fact that she is reading these letters. Her voice is in the service of her mother's words, leaving unsettled whether she is breaking free or failing to break free by reading them aloud.[52] Lugones came to realize that she had been grafting her mother's substance onto herself, whereas Anzaldúa came to realize that she had to resist her mother in order to become herself. By the time Akerman makes *News from Home*, she is voicing something else: that her mother is absorbing her person, consuming her world. It is no coincidence that Akerman's films from here on out become increasingly explicitly devoted to her mother. Behind them lingers the suspicions that it is her mother that fills out her substance, making her who she is, imbuing her with a distinct point of view.

We might expect that the letters and the images will be running alongside one another, brought together by Akerman's experience of being pulled in two directions. But as the film unfolds, the passersby become illuminated by her feeling of in-betweenness conjured by the words and images. We see a man inside a pizza shop assembling a pie and placing it into an oven. People pass in front of his window, making him look as if inside a lit-up fishbowl, a specimen on display (Figure 3). He might be in-the-world, unreflectively at ease, with his pizza ready-to-hand, but we are viewing him through a layer that casts him in a different light. He is no longer familiar but estranged, a stranger stuck inside his narrow shop.

In one striking moment, the street scene and the letter read coincide. Akerman speaks the following lines: "I'm glad you like New York. People here are surprised. They say New York is terrible, inhuman. Perhaps they don't know it and are too quick to judge."

FIGURE 3 News from Home *directed by Chantal Akerman 1977. Collections CINEMATEK—© Fondation Chantal Akerman.*

While we hear these words, the frame is teeming with people going about their daily business, living alongside each other, not paying each other much heed (Figure 4). Although they seem to know their way around more competently and confidently than Akerman herself, they are mostly on their own. The more people pass across her field of vision, the more they start to look like lonely vagabonds. Does this make them inhuman or human? The coincidence of words and images goes even one step further. In a series of shots filmed at one intersection, the camera begins shifting from one angle to another, following the views from different streets. It is almost as if we are no longer limited by the vantage point of a human body but are watching the city view itself.[53]

FIGURE 4 News from Home *directed by Chantal Akerman 1977. Collections CINEMATEK—© Fondation Chantal Akerman.*

Many have noted that the footage of the city seems impersonal. For instance, Margaret Iversen has argued that *News from Home* seeks to take Akerman out of the picture, for "[o]nce a personal subjective viewpoint is vacated, another reality can come into view."[54] But it is hard to think of a film less convinced that the personal subjective viewpoint can be vacated, and that if it is, any reality will still remain in view. Whenever Akerman takes herself out of the picture, it is in order to communicate the experience of someone who feels absent from the place where they live, thereby demonstrating that they are anything but absent from this very place.

There is one image in which Akerman is even visually present, a lengthy shot that includes a dim reflection with Babette Mangolte in the window of a subway car. Their bodies do not move, but their reflection flickers. They appear as ghostly shapes, makers of this film but also passengers on this train, as anonymous as anyone. This shot alone leaves little doubt about the film's point of view as the view of someone now perched in the middle, in between a home to which she cannot return and a home at which she cannot arrive. The final image in *News from Home* is the only shot that includes Manhattan's recognizable skyline, cloaked in fog. For the duration of seven minutes, we are on the Staten Island Ferry, surrounded by seagulls, succumbing to an eastward pull.[55]

## Porous Walls

*D'Est*, filmed in 1992 and released in 1993, tracks a movement from the east to an even farther east. It begins in a summery East Germany, moves through Poland, Lithuania, and Ukraine, ending in Moscow in the dead of winter. The Berlin Wall has recently fallen, and the USSR is about to dissolve. According to a statement that Akerman wrote, she wanted "to make a grand journey through Eastern Europe while there is still time," recording everything that moved her on the way: "Faces, streets, cars going by and buses, train stations and plains, rivers, and oceans, streams and brooks, trees and forests, interiors, doors, windows, meals being prepared. Women and men, young and old, people passing by or at rest, seated or standing, even lying down. Days and nights, wind and rain, snow and springtime."[56]

*D'Est* recalls aspects of her earlier works. Marion Schmid compares it to *Hotel Monterey*, featuring people who are "stoically bearing the camera gaze without returning it."[57] Its street scenes, especially of people crossing paths on busy corners or cars rushing in the direction of the camera, resemble those from *News from Home*. But there is a marked departure, for Akerman is taking a decisive step in the direction of "world"-traveling to her subjects. For one, these are no longer ghostly shapes. By focusing her attention on their faces and their bodies, she is showing them as real people, even if she continues to maintain a respectful distance from their lives. For another, these are no longer lonely vagabonds. By switching back and forth between individuals and groups, she gives both sides their due.[58] Though the people in *D'Est* do appear unmoored and at times even isolated, Akerman emphasizes a social connectedness that goes beyond her earlier films.

The experience of watching *D'Est* has been described as disorienting.[59] The film contains very little information. There is no voiceover, instead a non-synchronous soundtrack composed of traffic, murmurings, songs, and a cello, filmed live and then remixed in the studio. The film itself does not offer the context that would be needed to interpret what we are seeing in its full significance, providing only minimal clues to specific locations. Unless you recognize these places or understand these languages, the world shown will be barely legible. The same cannot be said of the people featured in the film. Their world remains legible to them, at least for now. Although the film includes no interviews, we as viewers are being led into their experience of this moment. We hear people greeting each other, getting into squabbles. We witness quotidian scenes: a man eating his lunch at a kitchen table, a couple playing cards by the sea, a young girl applying lipstick, people knitting or reading at a railway station, and a woman cutting up sausage and bread into thick slices in her kitchen.

An especially poignant scene is set in a ballroom. While a singer sings a wistful tune, a couple appears on the dancefloor, dancing with abandon (Figure 5). These people carry on with their daily lives despite the fact that they have every reason to expect that the social fabric they took for granted is unraveling. I was reminded of a passage from Goethe's *Elective Affinities*: "So all in their different fashions pursued their daily lives, thoughtfully or not; everything seemed to be following its usual course, as is the way in monstrously strange circumstances when everything is at stake: we go on with our lives as though nothing were the matter."[60] The people in *D'Est* live in an unstable moment, suspended between a vanishing past and an accelerating future.[61] What else is there to do but to go on with your life as if nothing is happening?

*D'Est* visualizes this combination of reflecting and not reflecting to which Goethe alludes. I think that it would be a mistake to assume that

FIGURE 5 D'Est *directed by Chantal Akerman 1993. Collections CINEMATEK—© Fondation Chantal Akerman.*

continuing in the face of pending change is like sticking your head in the sand. Akerman might even describe it as a form of resistance. She tells the story of a resistance that moved her, her father refusing to get off a train even though he was sitting across from an SS officer.[62] These small gestures might look like little nothings. But she thinks that even when they do not change the course of history, they preserve shreds of meaning. Through their postures, movements, and expressions, the people in *D'Est* are holding onto such shreds, but also expressing an awareness of an approaching unknown. Whether they are standing on sidewalks or walking down roads, the impression they make is one of apprehension, of waiting to see what comes next. *D'Est* is pervaded by scenes of seemingly interminable waiting. The camera pans across crowds waiting for transportation that never arrives. The camera also fixes on groups walking across its field of vision, wherefrom or whereto we never find out. In one of its opening shots, we face a man looking uneasy and impatient, smoking on a bench.[63] Many of the people in the film notice that they are being filmed, though they tend to bear it with the same stoicism as those who granted Akerman permission to enter their homes. Whether alone or together, they are powerlessly biding their time, not just because they do not know what is in store for them, but also because they cannot do anything about it. The conditions for daily life are not in their hands.

According to Akerman's statement, she was drawn to Eastern Europe for two reasons. One was personal: her mother's family had emigrated to Brussels from a town in Poland, though Akerman avoided the return to her roots and steered clear of her mother's hometown. The other was historical: soon these countries would go their separate ways and be transformed by capitalism, though here too, she avoided making assumptions. As she puts it, "I will not attempt to show the disintegration of a system, nor the difficulties of entering into another one, because she who seeks shall find, find all too well, and end up clouding her vision with her own preconceptions."[64] But the editing process revealed something she did not expect to find. Although she had followed her feeling, this feeling had been guided by ingrained images not immediately apparent to her. She noticed a pattern emerging out of the footage, shot upon shot of people huddled together or lying in train station corridors. There is a long tracking shot inside a station platform in which the camera is placed so low that it cuts off people's heads, gliding across their visually decapitated bodies (Figure 6).

The footage recalled what she describes as a primal scene etched in her memory.[65] "All images of evacuations, of walking in the snow with

FIGURE 6 D'Est *directed by Chantal Akerman 1993. Collections CINEMATEK—© Fondation Chantal Akerman.*

packages toward an unknown place, of faces and bodies placed one next to the other, of faces flickering between robust life and the possibility of a death which would strike them down without having asked for anything. And it is always like that. Yesterday, today, and tomorrow."[66] When she was done making the film, she said to herself: *"that's* what it was: once again *that."*[67] The film resounds with echoes, contesting that the present could be detached from the past.[68] Since these echoes are not explicit in the film, it is possible to watch it and miss them, though I would think that they are amplified by the lack of information Akerman provides. It makes *D'Est* more than a record of a specific time and place. It captures what Akerman takes to be true of yesterday, today, and tomorrow, that to be an individual in historical time is to be vulnerable to forces that can wipe your world (any world) away.[69]

If *D'Est* is a film about the permeability between past and present, *From the Other Side* is a film about the permeability between two contemporary worlds, the United States and Mexico, countries that share a border demarcated by a wall.[70] Akerman is showing the wall from both points of view, the first part of the film from the Mexican side, the second part from the US side. Although "other" is a relative term, *From the Other Side* is definitely taking a side.[71] Once again, it was both personal and historical reasons that drew Akerman to this region. In her words, "I wanted to go to the American-Mexican border because I read an article in the newspaper and was struck by the words used by one of the Americans who was quoted in the article: one word he used was 'dirt'—'They're going to bring dirt.' That made me think of the other times in history when the word 'dirt' was used."[72]

The documentary was also motivated by a new policy implemented after 9/11 that cracked down on illegal immigration in urban areas, effectively forcing migrants into the desert where they were less likely to survive. This policy is even discussed in the film. A local Arizona sheriff claims that "from every aspect it was a bad strategy and a bad plan," and Akerman adds that the person who devised it was clearly "never hungry" if she believed that this policy would discourage people from risking their lives.[73] The film can be said to commemorate those lost in the desert, those whose bodies were never found. They are the specters of *From the Other Side*, hovering somewhere in the arid landscapes Akerman patiently documents. The film concludes with a negative shot, archival footage from Border Patrol, of a line of white shapes (Figure 7). After this haunting image, Akerman reads a fictional text (usually interpreted as the film's "coda") about a mother who successfully crosses the border only to disappear into the crowd.[74]

FIGURE 7 From the Other Side *directed by Chantal Akerman 2002. Collections CINEMATEK—© Fondation Chantal Akerman.*

Akerman inches even closer to her subjects, featuring not only their faces and bodies but also their words.[75] She presents how they view their own context or how they interpret their own experience.[76] Akerman also inserts herself into her film. We hear her asking questions in Spanish and in English. But her acoustic presence is hardly distracting. If anything, *From the Other Side* underscores that locating oneself in the film is not in tension with allowing the subject to reveal itself. Akerman is generous in her attention, letting people take as much time as they need to say what they have to say. Moreover, Akerman's love of the everyday makes room for other people's self-disclosure. She wants to hear whatever they are willing to reveal. Her interview with Delphina Maruri Miranda can be read along the lines of "world"-traveling in Lugones's sense. Akerman asks her about her deceased son and grandson, but Delphina immediately resists casting them as mere victims. Rather, she begins talking about her son's dreams for their town, about his ambitions to fix its infrastructure and to see the town grow, and about his love of working in the fields, a love he shared with his son. The impression we get is not only of a woman who doesn't want to lay her trauma bare, but also of a woman who insists on her son's attachment to his own community. By hearing her out, we are catching a glimpse of a world that is meaningful to her.

*From the Other Side* is about the "borderlands" in Anzaldúa's sense, a material and psychic reality created by a border in the land and a border in the mind.[77] For Anzaldúa, the borderlands are an indeterminate area forcefully circumscribed. Akerman is stressing this indeterminacy at an acoustic level, since so many of her shots are rather noisy. Babette Mangolte notes that in the tracking shots, "[w]hat we hear is a complex magma of white noises that call attention to the indecipherability of the world."[78] The film also features many images of the wall, an "open wound" cutting through an open desert.[79] They create the overall impression of an infinite wall, a wall that just keeps on going. What such images make so vivid is that the wall is an unnatural boundary, imposed arbitrarily through political and economic power. Such images also make vivid that this boundary creeps into the thinking not only of those that live nearby but of Americans and Mexicans more broadly. It has far-reaching implications for the worlds that are constituted by it and for the attitudes expressed by those who inhabit these worlds.

In Jonathan Rosenbaum's words, "which side of the border we're viewing it from can make all the difference."[80] Although Akerman interviews people on both sides, the asymmetries continue to mount. On the Mexican side, people exercise their agency by investing in the survival of individuals, families, and communities. On the American side, people exercise their agency in the defense of private property.

An early image in the film shows a hodgepodge wall, on our (Mexican) side a couple with a meandering child, on the other (American) side a pair of armed guards (Figure 8).

This difference is only exacerbated by an interview that Akerman conducts with a couple on the American side later in the film, a couple whose fears for their children and for themselves are imaginary. Even though they admit that there is no evidence to support this, they are afraid that Mexicans will bring fatal diseases into the United States. They speculate that there will not be enough vaccines for everyone so that parents like themselves will have to sacrifice for their children and grandchildren. The husband comments that he wouldn't mind, "I've had a great life." This offhand remark stands in stark contrast with another scene on the Mexican side, which features a group of migrants sitting in a restaurant. The man at the head of the table reads a collective statement that includes all of their names, concluding

FIGURE 8 From the Other Side *directed by Chantal Akerman 2002. Collections CINEMATEK—© Fondation Chantal Akerman.*

with the words, "some have it all, and others have nothing . . . from nothingness we come and to nothingness we will return."

## No Home Movie

Akerman's complicated relationship to the concept of home is most evident in her last documentary, *No Home Movie* (2015), composed of shots from the desert in Israel and from inside her mother's apartment in Brussels.[81] Akerman describes the film in both fictional and nonfictional terms: "The red thread of this film is a character, a woman born in Poland, who arrives in Belgium in 1938 to flee the pogroms and the horror. This woman is my mother. Within and solely within her apartment in Brussels."[82] The combination of title and subject suggests an identification of "home" and "mother." Her mother not only symbolizes home to her—Nelly is home. This can mean that Akerman only feels fully at home in her mother's company or at her mother's place. It can also mean that Akerman regards her mother as the basis for her being-in-the-world more generally, maybe even as the source of her world's meaning. The world that is readily intelligible to Akerman needn't shrink to the size of her mother's apartment, but it might be the case that she can only feel at home elsewhere as long as she remains connected to her mother. In the final shot of the film, which is an almost completely immobile image, we see what has remained of this home after her mother's death: an empty room overladen with grief. But it is not completely empty. Akerman casts a shadow onto a vase.

*No Home Movie* is the documentary in which Akerman is most fully included. We hear her, see her, and listen to stories told about her past and present. In many scenes, she is even a body moving around her mother's space as if it were her own. If *News from Home* gives voice to the suspicion that Akerman hasn't separated from her mother, by *No Home Movie* this is no longer a genuine threat because Akerman clearly leads a full life of her own. Even once her mother is gone, Akerman is still in the apartment, tying her shoes, leaving the room.[83]

But there are also shots that counter Akerman's embodied presence on the screen, for instance, her silhouette on the flickering surface of opaque waters (Figure 9). She seems to be turning ghostly in her own eyes, which can give the impression that we are now given access to her inner life.[84] As Kate Zambreno writes of *No Home Movie*, "How to represent privacy and sadness in a work. The daughter is the camera. The camera is the daughter. I sense the grieving daughter, editing this work, pausing, watching her mother in decline. Her presence and then her absence."[85] Since Akerman is so often shown on the screen

FIGURE 9 No Home Movie *directed by Chantal Akerman 2015. Collections CINEMATEK—© Fondation Chantal Akerman.*

alongside her mother, much of the footage couldn't have been taken from the daughter's literal point of view, but from the point of view of some object in the room. Later in the film, Akerman's camera also records Akerman filming her mother with what looks like a handheld camcorder. But such static shots are balanced by sequences recorded while Akerman is holding the camera, sequences that seem more revealing of her state of mind. With her, we stumble through a dark hallway on our way from the kitchen to the bathroom. With her, we watch the desert from a bumpy car ride. What makes these sequences so affecting is the feeling they convey of Akerman disoriented and unanchored.

*No Home Movie* is a film about homecoming. Since Akerman films most of it inside her mother's apartment in Brussels, the term "home" conjures an association with a private space, a space insulated from a broader context. But the film also includes images of people hanging out in the park, the wind whipping a tree in the desert, noisy traffic, and breezy meadows.[86] When placed alongside *News from Home*, *No Home Movie* seems to complete a classic tale, a young woman leaving home in search of herself and then returning to the home she left behind, from which her mother kept beckoning her in the earlier letters. There are even striking similarities between the two films. In a later scene, while talking to her other daughter (Sylviane), Nelly complains that Akerman doesn't tell her anything about her life, or at least nothing of importance. Akerman and her mother are seen together in the kitchen discussing her mother's favorite subjects from the earlier letters: health, relatives, and so on. The two women are finally shown next to each other, talking to each other while simultaneously on the screen, rather than competing for authorship. Akerman can be said to have traveled to her mother's "world," indulging her mother's priorities, listening to whatever is on her mother's mind.

*No Home Movie* can also be read as a film about the impossibility of homecoming, as well as about the limits of traveling to another's "world." Akerman is only sometimes at her mother's apartment. Frequently she is on the road, calling her on Skype from locations as far-flung as Oklahoma. This indicates that Akerman has hardly abandoned her vagabond life that started when she first moved to New York decades ago. During their Skype conversations, Nelly asks why she is filming her onscreen, and Akerman answers, "I want to show you that there is no distance in the world" and "I want to show you how small the world is," but the mediated way in which they communicate, their inability to hear each other without interruption, and her mother's frustrated desire to hold her daughter in her arms tell a different story. Heidegger criticized technology for eliminating all meaningful distances, distances that are integral to our having a meaningful world. By talking to her mother on Skype, has Akerman erased the very difference between home and elsewhere? And if so, would erasing this difference mean that she now feels at home everywhere, or does it mean that everywhere—including her home—has become an elsewhere?

The title of *No Home Movie* includes a negation. Its first word is a "No." According to one reading, the title is claiming that this is not a *home movie*, something artlessly homemade.[87] It includes references to a larger natural and even political context. It is arguably as stylized as Akerman's earlier documentaries, and some of its home-movie-like scenes even recall Akerman's structural and minimalist films like *Hotel Monterey*. For instance, there are moments in which the mother's face on the computer screen dissolves into a sea of pixels, turning into abstract shapes and patterns. According to another reading, the title is claiming that this is a movie about *no-home*, about not being at home, or about the absence of home. It seems to me like this would suggest something other than erasing the distinction between home and elsewhere, and in this way obviating the concept of home. The film keeps running up against one ineradicable barrier to homecoming, which is also an ineradicable barrier to "world"-traveling, a wall that Akerman cannot cross. Her home, her mother, is slipping away, descending down a solitary path. For a split second, a reflection of Akerman on her computer screen comes into focus just as her mother's image begins to blur (Figure 10).[88]

In my interpretation of Akerman's documentaries, I have emphasized her effort to arrive at the concept of home negatively, via what it is not to be at home in the world. This effort comes to a head in *No Home Movie*. It isn't just that Akerman is no longer at home

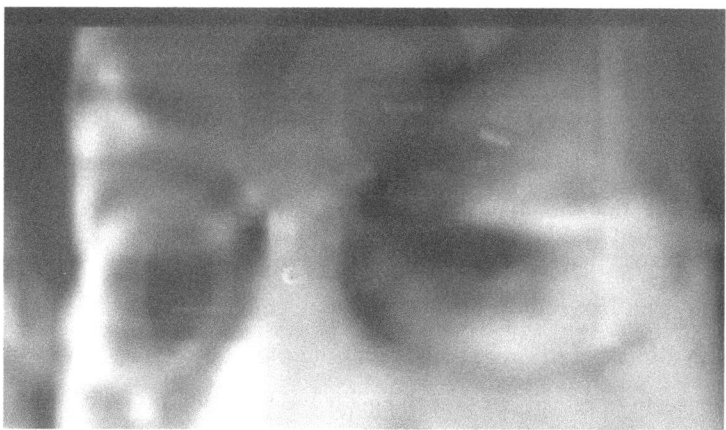

FIGURE 10 No Home Movie *directed by Chantal Akerman 2015. Collections CINEMATEK—© Fondation Chantal Akerman.*

at her mother's apartment in Brussels, since she comes only for the occasional visit. It is also that Nelly is, in a sense, not at home there either or not as at home as we might have expected.[89] Nelly conceals quite a bit behind her familiarity. Although she is moving around her space for the most part with ease, at least in the first half of the film, Akerman's camera catches her in moments of pensive silence, during which we are led to wonder to which places (and memories) her mind goes. Akerman makes her last and best effort to pose this question without violating Nelly's privacy. She involves her mother in conversations about Poland, the Second World War, the Belgian king. She alludes to the Holocaust without asking Nelly to discuss it, though she does later say to one of the caretakers that Nelly had been in Auschwitz, adding that this is "why my mother is like that," as if offering an explanation. In this way, Akerman's specific interest in the theme of home and its absence revisits her larger concern with the challenge of filming another person's inner life.

Akerman remembers something Nelly once told her. They were exiting the theater after a screening of Akerman's latest film when Nelly said, "you have all that, and I had only Auschwitz." According to Akerman, "I realized that same moment that I could not speak on her behalf, she was the only one who could speak, and if she didn't want to speak, that should be *it*."[90] *No Home Movie* is the culmination of her acceptance that there are things about her mother that she will never know, no matter how attentively she documents her. Although the film also aspires to register a universal unknowability, audiences did not seem to get this, or they did get it and were not interested. Either way, they filed out of theaters in droves. Akerman herself described her fear of them when she realized that she had shown something so intimate to an unreceptive crowd.[91] Whether or not others recognized themselves, *No Home Movie* tackles this unbridgeable divide with grace and restraint. We get up close only when Nelly is on Akerman's computer screen. Otherwise, we catch indirect sights through doorways, curtains, via the back of her head, via a face occluded by the afternoon light. A poignant image is of a bright blue lounge chair lying in the backyard.[92] As the camera keeps returning to the chair throughout the film, we begin to suspect that this dispatch from the outer world should tell us something about what is happening inside the apartment, inside the people inside the apartment, though what exactly is hard to put into words.

# Notes

1   Two of these documentaries (*D'Est* and *From the Other Side*) are usually grouped together (along with *Sud* and *Là-Bas*) as being about a sense of "place." Terms like "home" are also often brought into connection with them. See, for example, Babette Mangolte, *Selected Writings*, p. 241.

2   Sandy Flitterman-Lewis argues that "home" as a concept is both "elusive" and "impossible" and that this attitude is rooted in Akerman's Jewish identity ("Ephemeral, Elusive, Impossible").

3   Pajama Interview.

4   Quoted in Margulies, *Nothing Happens*, p. 42.

5   Irene Valle Corpas: "In her cinema, time, bodies and the places through which they glide, were gazed at directly, face to face, as political elements" ("Between Home and Flight," p. 3).

6   Her documentaries are sometimes described as "phenomenological." It is a term that Akerman often applied to her own films, including her fictional works.

7   The exception is *Sud*. In this documentary, Akerman travels to Jasper, Texas, to document the immediate aftermath of the brutal and racist murder of

James Bird, Jr. It is perhaps Akerman's most controversial documentary, and it was also the one in which she is least present.

8   From *Chantal Akerman, From Here*. "After a documentary is shot and edited, if it does not open a breach into the imaginary, if fiction does not slip into it, then, for me, it is not a documentary. As for fiction, if no documentary aspects slip into it, then I find it difficult to think of it as a fiction film" (*Autoportrait*, p. 89; translated by Schmid).

9   Her early fictional films are self-conscious in the sense that Akerman casts herself in the main role.

10  Cavell, *The World Viewed*, p. 127.

11  Ibid., pp. 127–8.

12  Pajama Interview.

13  Quoted in Jonathan Rosenbaum, "Place and Displacement."

14  Rosenbaum, "Place and Displacement": "about the states of Akerman's consciousness, her thoughts and feelings of displacement or alienation, in relation to those places."

15  Maria Lugones, "Purity, Impurity, and Separation," p. 469.

16  Amy Taubin, "Bordering on Documentary."

17  I will focus only on *Being and Time*, but in his later writings Heidegger employs many home-related terms: *Heim, Zuhause, Wohnen*.

18  Quoted in Andreas Elpidorou and Lauren Freeman, "Affectivity in Heidegger I," p. 665.

19  For more on Heidegger's conception of moods, see Elpidorou and Freeman, "Affectivity in Heidegger I"; and Sacha Golob, "Methodological Anxiety: Heidegger on Moods and Emotions."

20  Mariana Ortega, *In Between*, p. 12.

21  Ortega rejects a picture of these worlds as complete and self-enclosed, insulated from each other. She takes herself to be taking up Maria Lugones's notion of "worlds" as interdependent.

22  See also Ortega, *In Between*, pp. 49–50.

23  Anzaldúa, *Borderland*, p. 25.

24  "Borders are set up to define the places that are safe and unsafe, to distinguish *us* from *them*" (Anzaldúa, *Borderland*, p. 25).

25 Ortega calls this "hometactics" (pp. 201–10).

26 Ortega criticizes Lugones on this point: "It is another chapter in yet another unfortunate dichotomy of public/private that Lugones also wishes to dismantle on her analysis of tactical strategies" (p. 205).

27 Lugones:

> For something to be a "world" in my sense, it has to be inhabited at present by some flesh and blood people. That is why it cannot be a utopia. It may also be inhabited by some imaginary people. It may be inhabited by people who are dead or people that the inhabitants of this "world" met in some other "world" and now have in this "world" in imagination. "Playfulness, 'World'-Travelling, and Loving Perception" (pp. 9–10).

28 Lugones, "Playfulness, 'World'-Travelling, and Loving Perception" p. 3.

29 Ibid.

30 A "world"-traveler in her sense is never to be confused with an expat or a tourist (Ibid., 19).

31 According to Ortega, Lugones did not consider the dangers internal to this practice, that "world"-travel lapses into another routine, or that loving perception damages its object. Although Ortega adopts a version of Lugones's proposal, she argues that we need to become critical world-travelers, travelers who are "critical about the worlds to which one travels and about one's own practice of world-traveling" (Ortega, *In-Between Latina Feminist Phenomenology, Multiplicity, and the Self*, p. 138).

32 Her point is that even those who are marginalized can succumb to arrogant perception.

33 Lugones, "Playfulness," p. 8.

34 Anzaldúa, *Borderlands*, p. 38.

35 Sitney cites four characteristics: fixed camera position, the flicker effect, loop printing, and re-photography off the screen, though it was rare that a film would include all four.

36 Margaret Iversen, "World Without a Self," argues that Akerman is using tracking shots in order to give the viewer the impression of a world without a self. "Several sections are filmed from moving vehicles, including cars, subways, trains and the Staten Island Ferry" (p. 755). The idea is that moving vehicles introduce contingency—you film whatever happens to be there, independently of you.

37  Lugones wants to locate the theoretical perspective in the spatiality of the street, thereby overcoming the division between theory and practice. The theorist is someone who looks for hang-out spots and participates in them by hanging out.

38  Pajama Interview.

39  She had already directed *Jeanne Dielman* and received a grant to make the film.

40  For a discussion of the larger implications of Akerman's decision to document from her own height, see Kristine Butler, "Bordering on Fiction: Chantal Akerman's *From the East*," p. 163.

41  There are two striking examples: in *Hotel Monterey*, two men see her in the elevator and step back, even though the elevator is otherwise empty; in *News from Home*, a man in a green shirt gets onto the subway car and stares at the camera for a few minutes before switching to another car.

42  Babette Mangolte Interview on Criterion Channel.

43  According to Marion Schmid, this is a pessimistic conclusion to the film: "A grey ashen morning rises over the housing estate of upper Broadway. The iconic New York of glittering boulevards and elegant skyscrapers is a far removed, barely fathomable reality" (*Chantal Akerman*, p. 25).

44  On the podcast "The Akerman Year," the participants settle on the term "overlived" to describe the space.

45  As Corpas notes, the individuals that Akerman films "do not do anything, they do not move, they limit themselves to being there and the spectator waits with them for the time to pass" ("Between Home and Flight," p. 11).

46  Kate Zambreno, *Drifts*, p. 80.

47  Ivone Margulies in *Nothing Happens* traces this influence of minimalism on Akerman's work.

48  "Getting Ready for the Golden Eighties," an interview with Gary Indiana: https://www.artforum.com/features/getting-ready-for-the-golden-eighties-a-conversation-with-chantal-akerman-208022/.

49  *News from Home* also made it onto the 2022 *Sight and Sound* poll in fifty-second place. It has two soundtracks, both read by Akerman (one in French and one in English).

50  Jennifer Baker, "The Feminine Side of New York," argues that Akerman's position in space suggests a creative act of "dwelling" that stands in contrast with the creativity associated with architecture (pp. 41–2).

51 Zambreno observes: "The exterior shots are the postcards [Akerman] does not send" (*Drifts*, p. 291).

52 In the Pajama Interview, Akerman says about the film: "I love it. Still not free from my mother." She asks: "Am I conscious of being an individual? I know that I'm just myself, even though I don't know what it means to be oneself."

53 Kenneth White ("Urban Unknown") has pointed out that this specific footage is filmed at New York's geographical center, the corner of 5th Avenue and 46th Street: "But Akerman is not a New Yorker. News from Home is the product of an individual on uneasy terms with her environment." He claims that we see this uneasiness in the fact that Akerman sticks so closely to New York's grid, allowing it to dictate the sequence of shots. He has also argued that the scholarship on this film underplays the importance of New York as the location, making it seem as if it were simply an incidental site of anxiety.

54 Iversen, "World Without a Self," p. 758. Iversen argues that Akerman is following in Edward Hopper's footsteps in filming a world without a self. But she also points out that such self-less scenes invite a mood of alienation or mourning because they make you think of a world that will survive your own death. If your view of a world without a self is shaped by such a mood, are you really seeing a world without a self?

55 Maria Walsh reads this final shot as a "freedom from identity" ("News from Home the Redux Version"); Griselda Pollock reads it as a "journey towards maternal trauma" ("The Long Journey"); Jerry White describes it as "passionate and almost climactic" ("Akerman's Revisionist Aesthetic," p. 54).

56 This is from an essay Akerman wrote to accompany an installation made from the film: "Bordering on Fiction: Chantal Akerman's *D'Est*."

57 Marion Schmid, *Chantal Akerman*, p. 24.

58 In her self-statement, Akerman claims that she was more interested in "faces" than in "souls." She also noted in the Pajama Interview that she was influenced by Levinas's views about the ethical significance of a face-to-face encounter and that confronting a face is disarming and rules out killing the other.

59 Marion Schmid, "A visual metaphor for the frequent territorial changes the region underwent in its tormented past, this lack of spatial demarcation, together with the film's disjointed narrative structure, creates a sense of disorientation that, from the outset, taints the viewing experience" (p. 103).

60 Goethe, *Elective Affinities*, p. 89.

61 Marion Schmid: "Suspended between past and future, between the collapse of Communism and an as yet uncertain new order, Eastern Europeans, in Akerman's cinematic language, become a community of wandering souls, nomads without a fixed destiny" (p. 104).

62 Pajama Interview.

63 According to Claire Atherton, "Chantal liked frontal shots. It was not a formal decision but a taste, almost a need. The frontal axis does not describe, does not designate, but creates a space of perception and reflection." http://www.sensesofcinema.com/2015/chantal-akerman/chantal-akerman-claire-atherton/.

64 From "Bordering on Fiction." She adds, "This undoubtedly will happen anyway; it can't be helped. But it will happen indirectly."

65 Marion Schmid relates this to Benjamin's concept of the dialectical image, in which a past that isn't directly represented becomes visible. Benjamin's "dialectical" relationship between the present and the past was clearly of interest to Akerman. In *Autoportrait* she writes: "The way in which the past received the imprint of a higher present event is determined by the *image* in which it is contained. And this dialectical penetration, this capacity to render present past correlations, is the test of truth of the present action" (Quoted in Schmid, *Chantal Akerman*, p. 113).

66 "Bordering on Fiction."

67 Quoted in Schmid, *Chantal Akerman*, p. 107.

68 As Alisa Lebow puts it, "these memories are hiding behind or in front of or just beneath every image she records" ("Memory Once Removed," p. 49).

69 Schmid describes the film as "a work replete with memory, but which eschews explicit commemoration and one which, through its haunted images of destitution, warns of humanity's fragility before the vagaries of History," p. 107.

70 Akerman also made installations from her footage for both films, which raises different questions about the role of the spectator.

71 She admits this in *Autoportrait*.

72 Interview with Scott MacDonald.

73 She was talking about Doris Meissner, the former commissioner of the Immigration and Naturalization Service.

74 Rosenbaum: "Akerman traces some of her jobs and finds oblique references to her in the stray comments of other people, following the woman's elusive trajectory as if she were a ghost fading into an anonymity of the hypnotic superhighway."

75 According to her cinematographer Robert Fenz, Akerman didn't want to include interviews but was urged to do so by her producer Thierry Garrel (specifically because there were no interviews in *D'Est*). See Albertine Fox, "Vocal Landscapes," p. 115.

76 Jonathan Rosenbaum, "Place and Displacement," claims that in *From the Other Side* Akerman "goes well beyond sympathetic tourism," of which he accuses *Sud*.

77 Albertine Fox compares this film and Anzaldua's text in "Vocal Landscapes."

78 Mangolte, *Selected Writings*, p. 241.

79 Rosenbaum: "The wall that appeared to be a neutral dividing line at the beginning of the film seems more and more like a scar once we see the kinds of pain and anguish it causes" ("Place and Displacement").

80 Ibid.

81 The other contender would have been *Là-Bas* (2006). Akerman was asked to make a documentary about Israel, and she ended up shooting this film almost entirely in a darkened apartment in Tel Aviv, mostly watching her neighbors through the blinds. Akerman's complicated relationship with Israel can be seen as a more concrete expression of her complicated relationship to the concept of home.

82 http://www.sensesofcinema.com/2015/chantal-akerman/chantal-akerman-claire-atherton/.

83 Alisa Lebow: "So when the filmmaker, who famously never ties her shoes, ties her shoes toward the end of No Home Movie, the scene falsely resolves that which was never going to be resolved, or perhaps it resolves it all too well" ("Identity Slips," p. 55).

84 The mood of the film does not necessarily correspond to Akerman's mood while shooting or editing the film. According to Claire Atherton, Akerman was calm and happy (see Ivone Margulies, "Elemental Akerman," fn 13).

85 Zambreno, *Appendix Project*, p. 127.

86 Akerman was taking a trip to Israel when she found out that her mother was dying, so she decided to include some of the footage she brought back. For a discussion of how these images of the desert help frame the film, see Margulies, "Elemental Akerman." Although Akerman includes no references to specific locations, Margulies argues that it matters to the film that these are images of Israel. It allows Akerman to place the personal in a political context. "Beginning with the shot of a battered tree, these images of a barren outdoors are the counterpoint without which the film might have never existed except as an amorphous home movie, a soothing filmic hearth" ("Elemental Akerman," p. 65).

87 According to Claire Atherton, Akerman wanted to call the film "Home Movie" in order to call to mind associations with homemade movies. But then Akerman decided that "No Home Movie" would be even more effective. Atherton comments: "That's the way she was thinking, always very quick and deep" (https://www.filmcomment.com/blog/interview-claire-atherton/).

88 Kate Rennebohm reads this moment in the film as joyful: "A solution through dissolution, this image is rapturous—a shimmering giggle of a stolen moment" (La Ressasseuse, p. 9.).

89 In an interview, Akerman mentions that this is in fact not her childhood home—her parents moved into this apartment relatively recently: https://mubi.com/en/notebook/posts/chantal-akerman-discusses-no-home-movie.

90 Ibid.

91 Ibid.

92 For a discussion of the significance of the blue lounge chair, see Ivone Margulies, "Elemental Akerman."

# 2

# Work

## In the Kitchen

It is in the kitchen that Akerman's life as a film director truly began. Her first film, *Blow Up My Town* (1968), features Akerman herself in the role of a teenager, who wreaks havoc with the supplies she finds inside cupboards before lighting a match and draping herself across a stove. The first film for which she became widely known, *Jeanne Dielman* (1975), has been described as an "ethnography of the kitchen crossed with classic tragedy."[1] *Jeanne Dielman* seems as if to start from the point at which *Blow Up My Town* ended, with the sound of gas accompanying its opening credits, its first image that of Jeanne standing over a stove, lighting a match.[2] But it goes on to tell a different story, not that of a teenager blowing things up but that of a housewife maintaining a strict routine. There are many differences between the two films. The first is a thirteen-minute short, the second three hours and twenty-one minutes long; the first anarchic in spirit, the second tightly wound; the first suffused with a fretful energy, the second excruciatingly patient. The last shot of *Jeanne Dielman* alone lasts seven minutes. But the two films have more in common than the look of the kitchen in which their central characters spend so much of their time on screen. In Akerman's words, "almost all of *Jeanne Dielman* was there in this first film."[3]

Their most obvious similarity is that both films are about housework, a combination of activities in the service of maintaining a domestic order. For some people, performing this work is a full-time, unpaid job. For others, it is a "second shift" after the paid work is finished. And still others are paid to perform it at other people's places of residence. While the social and political conditions under which housework is performed vastly differ, the activities themselves seem similar across the board. First, housework is, for the most part, monotonous, not offering a lot of variety from one day to the next. When creative activities like cooking are absorbed into one's household routine, even they tend to become unvaried. Second, housework has an important function to perform by meeting the needs of the members of one's households and preventing a home from deteriorating into a mess. Whoever it is that performs housework makes it possible for others to venture comfortably, well clothed and well fed, to their various destinations. Third, housework tends to be largely invisible, much of it taken for granted as occurring behind the scenes. Housework is not often recognized as work and even when it is remunerated, it is undervalued. This was true when Akerman directed *Blow Up My Town* and *Jeanne Dielman*. It remains true today. The fact that it is still so startling to watch a film that shows housework in meticulous detail surely contributes to *Jeanne Dielman*'s continuing hold.[4]

Akerman's project to make housework visible on film converged with feminist efforts to make housework visible in other domains.[5]

The feminist movement of the mid-1970s wanted to turn the light on housework and show it to be an especially fraught and especially neglected dimension of women's daily lives. To cite one example, the same year that *Jeanne Dielman* was released, Martha Rosler made "Semiotics of the Kitchen," a six-minute video in which Rosler names the utensils in a kitchen in alphabetical order and demonstrates their use through spiky and jerky gestures. Rosler was quite clear that "Semiotics of the Kitchen" is intended to be a feminist work of art. According to Rosler, "As the woman speaks, she names her own oppression."[6] There are even moments in *Jeanne Dielman* that call Rosler to mind or moments in "Semiotics of the Kitchen" that call Jeanne Dielman to mind. Just like Rosler uses an ice pick in a mildly menacing manner, so Jeanne Dielman reaches decisively for a pair of scissors lying on her dresser, turning it into a weapon.[7] This makes it all the more surprising that Akerman often denied that *Jeanne Dielman* should be interpreted as a feminist film. She seems to have worried that it would imply that Jeanne is a typical woman, rather than a singular individual in a highly specific predicament.[8]

In rejecting the label of feminist film, Akerman also wanted to emphasize that *Jeanne Dielman* is not narrowly about a woman's situation. Rather, it uses a woman's situation in order to address a broader tendency. Akerman claims that she discovered it in the particular story she was telling, again by moving from the concrete to the abstract, rather than the other way around: "At the beginning, I thought I was simply telling the story of three days in the life of a woman, but later I realized that it was a film about occupying time to avoid anguish, to keep moving so as not to think about the fundamental thing, which is being."[9] Akerman approaches Jeanne Dielman's predicament as an opportunity to investigate how a person comes to throw themselves so fully into a predictable life, a life constructed in such a way that there is no room for surprise.[10] She suggests that she could have made *Jeanne Dielman* about a man, though this would be overstating the case. In a sense, she proved the point with *Man with a Suitcase* (1984) a decade later. *Man with a Suitcase* is a film that revolves around a home-bound male character who is in some respects comparable to Jeanne Dielman because he keeps to a strict schedule that Akerman, as his unwilling roommate, is able to track. It is telling, however, that he does not perform a lot of housework beyond occasionally cleaning the dishes and once cooking ratatouille. We also have no reason to suspect that he is spending so much time inside the apartment because he is avoiding thinking about "being."

As Akerman eventually admitted, "I do think [*Jeanne Dielman*] is a feminist film because I give space to the things that were never, almost never, shown in that way, like the daily gestures of a woman . . . it's a feminist film—not just what it says but what is shown and how it is shown."[11] Initially Akerman worried that calling it a feminist film would imply that the film was critical of the life that Jeanne leads. But she came to see that it is her loving attention to Jeanne's daily gestures that makes this a feminist film. Akerman even suggests that *Blow Up My Town* is similarly loving, despite the different position it takes. She describes the relationship of the two films in the following way: "[*Blow Up My Town*], to me, is the opposite of *Jeanne Dielman*: the story of a girl who talks back to her mother, who explodes the norms confining women to womanly tasks, who breaks everything in [sic] kitchen and does everything in a crooked way—and yet, for all that, it is a love story: the film is dedicated."[12] As she put it, *Blow Up My Town* is a daughter's film, the story of a girl who talks back to her mother, even though we see no mother in it. This would make *Jeanne Dielman* a mother's film, the mother's version of the story. Or it is the version of the story that a daughter imagines her mother's to be.

In these two films, Akerman isolates the activities that constitute housework and takes them on their own terms. She seems less interested in the social and political conditions under which housework is performed and more interested in the activities themselves, their repetitive structure, and the way in which they do or do not engage the mind of the person performing them. The task of representing housework becomes a specific lens through which to address her bigger challenge of filming an inner life that is not expressed directly through speech. But as the divergences between the two films make clear, it makes a big difference which perspective you assume. In *Jeanne Dielman*, Akerman is approaching housework from the perspective of the person who performs it. In *Blow Up My Town*, she is approaching housework from the perspective of the person who does not (yet) perform it.

Though Akerman describes the two films as "opposites," she both invokes and undercuts another version of the inside-outside opposition. Here the insider perspective would be that of a woman who is already working in the kitchen and consumed by its demands. The outsider perspective would be that of a girl anticipating that the same fate awaits her, wishing to shed this burden before it is imposed. But both can be said to confront what it takes to represent housework in a way that is true to the work itself. It seems to be difficult and maybe undesirable to represent housework neutrally, without implicitly evaluating it by affirming it, criticizing it, or doing both at once. Given the mother-daughter context in which housework is often performed, observed, and remembered, the emotional stakes are inevitably high.

## The Value of Housework

Consider the following characterization of housework:

> Few tasks are more similar to the torment of Sisyphus than those of the housewife; day after day, one must wash dishes, dust furniture, mend clothes that will be dirty, dusty, and torn again. The housewife wears herself out running on the spot; she does nothing; she only perpetuates the present; she never gains the sense that she is conquering a positive good, but struggles indefinitely against evil. It is a struggle that begins again every day.[13]

This passage appears in Simone de Beauvoir's *The Second Sex*, published in 1949. In it, Beauvoir argues that femininity is not a set of natural attributes but a product of arduous and often "mutilating" socialization. In the words of its most famous sentence, *one is not born a woman but becomes one*. According to Beauvoir, girls are turned into women through a long process in which they are situated as the "other" in relation to a male "subject," which means that they are made to "submit to this foreign point of view."[14] Beauvoir is interested in capturing this subject-other structure that pervades the situation of women as women, but she is also interested in subverting it by entering into women's lived experience of their social roles. The second part of the book (called "Lived Experience") is a phenomenological description of "the girl," "the lesbian," "the married woman," and "the mother." This is also the part of the book in which we find the above characterization of housework, or the tasks of the housewife. Beauvoir takes herself to be approaching housework from the housewife's perspective. By doing so, she is treating her as the subject of her own life, someone who is not only subjected to external demands but has a lived experience of her social roles.

For Beauvoir, we can draw general and generally negative conclusions about the structure of housework. Its chores are for the most part identical day in day out, with no ultimate completion in sight. In short, housework is endlessly repetitive. She thinks that it is this fact alone that makes housework a kind of torment. Her point is not that housework is physically exhausting (though it often is) but that it is psychically frustrating.[15] Beauvoir thinks that housework has a structure in virtue of which it is incapable of yielding higher forms of satisfaction and of doing justice to the fact that it is performed by a conscious being. It must be done, there is no way around it, but it is simply too tedious and too fruitless to provide what she calls a "reason for living." Note that her criticism does not turn on the question of whether a woman has chosen or consented to take on the lion's share of this work. For Beauvoir, housework cannot be made into a meaningful project. Even though someone tasked with household maintenance might be motivated "to change this prison into a kingdom,"[16] she thinks that all such efforts are ultimately self-deceived. Beauvoir is describing housework in *The Second Sex*, thereby treating it as a subject matter that merits attention. But she is clearly casting housework in an unfavorable light.

Another term for endless repetition in Beauvoir's vocabulary is "immanence" (in contrast to "transcendence"), which has the following connotations: immanent activities (1) *reproduce life*: because housework is usually conjoined with raising children, Beauvoir considers it to be a service done to humanity as a biological species and so as bound to the life cycle; (2) *produce nothing enduring*: Beauvoir calls housework a merely negative activity in the sense of a battle *against* dirt, dust, disorder, and decay, which are enemies that cannot be permanently defeated.[17] This makes housework incapable of any lasting achievements;[18] (3) *produce nothing new*: she thinks that housework is eternally identical, for it does not transform the world beyond the home, nor do its activities substantially change from one generation to the next;[19] (4) *are mechanical:* housework for her is for the most part performed without thinking. Although it is sometimes accompanied by the pleasure of contemplation, this is so only during that fleeting instant when the work is finally done and the house temporarily spotless; (5) *are bound to the present*: housework traps a person in a never-ending present moment, foreclosing what she calls an "open future," which she understands through an analogy with an indeterminate horizon and considers to be a requirement for genuine freedom. Even though all human lives consist of a combination of immanence and transcendence, she thinks that it is in virtue of engaging in transcending activities that human beings raise themselves above the status of mere objects.

Beauvoir is aware that not every activity that belongs to housework will have the same endlessly repetitive structure. Cleaning is more mechanical than cooking, which you might think is capable of becoming a genuine project. Here Beauvoir points out that cooking is as frustrating as cleaning when it takes place inside the nuclear family, where it is taken for granted by one's husband and children.[20]

Because Beauvoir's discussion of housework is placed in her chapter on marriage, her assessment of housework must take the situation of the married woman into account. Since she concedes that all human lives will involve some degree of immanence, she is not arguing that immanence is to be avoided. Rather, what Beauvoir finds objectionable is to place the burden of immanence onto women in the way in which the institution of marriage has done.[21] But is housework so odious because it happens in the context of marriage or is rather marriage so odious because it burdens women with housework?[22] Since Beauvoir defines oppression as a condition of being trapped inside immanence, it seems as if she needs to appeal to the structure of household chores as such in order to make the case that marriage is an oppressive institution.[23] In the end, Beauvoir's criticism of housework is a part of her broader criticism of institutions that demand that some people devote themselves to immanence so that others are unburdened or untethered, free to pursue meaningful projects.

Beauvoir only had to observe her own mother to arrive at her negative assessment of both marriage and housework. As she puts it, "Her case alone would be enough to convince me that bourgeois marriage is an unnatural institution."[24] In *A Very Easy Death*, Beauvoir describes her mother's final days, her rage against death, and her attachment to life. It is a moving account of a mother-daughter reconnection. Beauvoir notes that her mother only came into her own once her husband had died and she was free to pursue projects that made her life meaningful to her. It was by marrying that Beauvoir's mother had renounced her aspirations, as well as surrendered the prospect of sexual satisfaction while in her prime. "A full-blooded, spirited woman lived on inside her, but a stranger to herself, deformed and mutilated."[25] Housework was part of the problem. As Beauvoir recounts, "When my father's circumstances changed and we experienced semi-poverty, Maman decided to look after the house without a servant. Unfortunately, housework bored her terribly, and she thought that she was lowering herself by doing it."[26] She was lowering herself in the sense that she was devoting her time to something that bored her, thereby giving up activities that would have been more fulfilling. But she was also lowering herself in the sense that she was taking on work that is usually reserved for servants, on whom she would have been happy to lean down for help. Her mother's attitude toward housework is clearly highly class specific. Is Beauvoir's as well?[27]

Several decades later, the connection between housework and class came under direct scrutiny through the Wages for Housework campaign, informing the background against which Akerman was making her films. Silvia Federici was a founding member of this campaign, which started as a grassroots movement in Italy in 1972 and remained active on an international scale until 1977. The campaign made the controversial demand that the state should pay a wage to those who perform housework, be it housewives, women for whom housework is a second shift, or anyone else doing it. This demand was met with considerable resistance from various corners, including the Left, so Federici undertook to clarify its basis. In her influential "manifesto" of 1975 called "Wages against Housework," she argues that the wage should not be considered an end in itself (or a "thing"), but rather a strategy for achieving a new perspective.[28] According to Federici, those who have already joined the campaign are not under the impression that providing women with "a lump of money" would solve their problems or transform their condition. Rather, they believe that a wage would expose aspects of housework that are otherwise hidden. She describes the demand for a wage as a perspective that women need to be able to assume toward their own work, making Wages for Housework a tool of feminist consciousness-raising.[29] It is also a perspective that is concerned with the place of housework in its social context. Her question is: what role does housework play in the world in which it is embedded?

First, the campaign makes clear that housework is a kind of work. It is depleting, deforming, and imposed as a duty. It is not a spontaneous act of love. Since housework's unwaged status has obscured this fact, demanding a wage for housework is a way of initiating a conceptual change and broadening the range of what gets counted as work. Second, the campaign holds that housework should be waged because it contributes to capitalist accumulation, creating surplus value by producing, nurturing, and disciplining workers.[30] This makes unpaid housework an instance of exploitation. But it is also no coincidence that housework has not been remunerated, placing it in the same category as other forms of unwaged labor on which capitalism has historically depended.[31] Third, the campaign shows that housework is not an expression of a natural attribute, something that women do out of an innate inclination. A wage would thus serve to denaturalize this work, to confirm that women who do it are already part of the working class, and to reveal that housework does not exhaust their identities as women. As Federici puts it,

> as soon as we raise our heads from the socks we mend and the meals we cook and look at the totality of our working day, we see

that while it does not result in a wage for ourselves, we nevertheless produce the most precious product to appear on the capitalist market: labor power. Housework is much more than house cleaning. It is servicing the wage earners physically, emotionally, sexually, getting them ready for work day after day.[32]

In sum, the Wages for Housework perspective places this work in its social context. Her arguments did not go unchallenged. In *Women, Race & Class*, Angela Davis takes on the central tenets of the Wages for Housework campaign. She denies that bourgeois housewives are in fact already members of the working class if they enjoy the economic privileges of their husbands. Davis also points out that Wages for Housework gives priority to the interests of the white housewife. Many women of color are employed to perform domestic chores and so are already receiving a wage for housework. According to Davis, the demand to wage housework does nothing to address the forms of exploitation that these women face.[33]

Federici diverges from Beauvoir on several fronts. First, while Beauvoir claimed that housework is fruitless, Federici holds that it does achieve something beyond a clean house. What it produces is a commodity, *labor power*, though seeing this requires "raising our head from the socks we mend," since it is not going to be self-evident to those who are in the midst of mending socks. Second, while Beauvoir holds that housework serves the biological species and remains unchanged from generation to generation, Federici argues that housework services capital and is thus affected by historically contingent conditions. Housework has been reshaped to produce workers who fit the demands of the capitalist market.[34] This means that housework is not an eternal recurrence of the same. Third, Federici does not share Beauvoir's measure of value. As we have seen, Beauvoir suggests that housework is less valuable (because less satisfying) than other work, specifically that with a transcending structure. Housework must be accomplished, but it cannot be a source of meaning and so cannot provide a reason for living. In contrast, Federici insists that the value of housework is in principle no different from the value of other work, even though its unwaged status proves that it has not been adequately valued. Her point is that housework has social value because it sustains not just the family unit, but the social world of which it is a part. Housework "keeps the world moving."[35]

That said, Federici was invested in dismantling housework by providing grounds for its refusal.[36] In her manifesto, which is titled "Wages *against* Housework," Federici writes,

> to demand wages for housework does not mean to say that if we are paid we will continue to do this work. It means precisely the opposite. To say that we want wages for housework is the first step towards refusing to do it, because the demand for a wage makes our work visible, which is the most indispensable condition to begin to struggle against it, both in its immediate aspect as housework and its more insidious character as femininity.[37]

According to Federici, a wage would show the women who are expected to perform housework that this is not their destiny, that they can refuse some of it, and maybe someday all of it. Federici is keen to avoid two mistakes. One would be to put housework on a pedestal and use its value as a reason to "send women back into the kitchen." The other would be to confuse the wage with the campaign's final goal.

According to Federici, the wage is a step in a revolutionary struggle that aims at the abolition of all wage labor. But her project raises unanswered questions. How does receiving a wage for housework constitute a step toward the abolition of wage labor? And what is the future of housework? Who will perform it after the revolution?

When Federici revisited her writings on housework decades later in preparing her volume *Revolution Point Zero*, she described her own trajectory as one from *refusal* to *valorization*.[38] Her early stance was to refuse housework completely. For example, Federici claims that for her and for many women of her generation, becoming a housewife represented a fate "worse than death."[39] She acknowledges an irony in her decision to devote her political and intellectual energies to defending its social value. But she eventually came to recognize other neglected aspects of housework as well. Like for Beauvoir, it is her mother's life that drew her attention to this kind of work and that inspired her to evaluate it. Federici recounts watching her mother with "great fascination":

> some of the most treasured memories of my childhood are of my mother making bread, pasta, tomato sauce, pies, liqueurs, and then knitting, sewing, mending, embroidering, and attending to her plants. I would some times help her in selected tasks, most often however with reluctance. As a child, I saw her work; later, as a feminist, I learned to see her struggle, and I realized how much love there had been in that work, and yet how costly it had been for my mother to see it so often taken for granted.[40]

In this passage, Federici is describing her mother's work in strikingly rich terms. This does not sound like the endless repetition of the soiled being made clean only to become soiled again, nor does it sound like simply an exploited service rendered to capital. Federici seems to be acknowledging something she had been reluctant to admit, that housework can also be an expression of love. While this observation does not speak against remunerating it, it suggests that there might be more to housework than is apparent to someone looking to reject it.

## Blow Up My Town

Akerman directed *Blow Up My Town* when she was eighteen years old, casting herself in the main and only role and shooting it inside her mother's actual kitchen. At first glance, the film seems to correspond to Federici's early stage of "refusal." A second glance suggests that it might also be an example of what Federici calls "valorization." Even though Akerman's character is obviously rejecting housework by doing it badly, the attitude of the film is affectionate and humorous. The film also expresses an inchoate sense of housework's broader significance. Just consider the fact that Akerman calls a film in which she is in effect blowing up a kitchen "blow up my town." She seems to be implying that to blow up the kitchen is to blow up the town.[41] The film also takes for granted a domestic order that the daughter then combusts. Although Akerman is the sole character in the film, she enters a tidy kitchen, which implies that the kitchen would have been tidied by someone prior to her arrival. The mother's presence is felt even if not seen. She is the "angel in the house," to borrow Virginia Woolf's famous phrase.

Here is the sequence of events: Akerman enters a high-rise building carrying flowers, picks up the mail, and pushes the elevator button only to bolt impatiently up the stairs before it even arrives. The camera shifts to the inside of a kitchen with two statements taped to the door: a poster with the words "Go Home" (accompanied by a smurf pointing a stern finger) and a piece of paper with the words "This is Me [*C'est Moi*]" (accompanied by a photograph of herself).[42] Akerman comes through the door, puts down the mail, and then attaches a letter to the handle of a cupboard. She spends a few seconds looking at the letter before taping the cracks of the kitchen door and taking bites from an apple. She boils pasta, eats it in great haste, and leaves the half-eaten plate on the floor, presumably for the cat to finish. She picks up the cat and throws her over the balcony. She steps onto the kitchen counter, throwing the contents of her cupboards around her and dropping cleaning powder into a container being filled with water in the sink. She dumps the water onto the floor, running a mop around the scattered items, before sitting down on the floor to polish her shoes. Is she cleaning the floor, dirtying

FIGURE 11 Blow Up My Town *directed by Chantal Akerman 1968. Collections CINEMATEK—© Fondation Chantal Akerman.*

it, or both? (Figure 11). It does not seem like Akerman is performing the chores usually done in the kitchen; she is deforming them. She takes a long look at herself in the mirror, covers her face with soap, and writes "All Is Over" with her soapy finger on the mirror. She burns the letter with a lit match and turns on the gas. After the screen has gone dark, we hear a series of bangs.

Housework is referenced obliquely as an unraveling routine. As Marion Schmid puts it, "Akerman parodies domestic cleaning rituals in a burlesque scene of inversion where the tasks habitually associated with creating order result in exactly the contrary: an ever-expanding mess."[43] Although Akerman's character does not seem to be interested in performing housework as it is usually done, the fact that she is doing such a bad job highlights the norms that govern the kitchen. These are norms that determine what it takes to perform activities such as cooking and cleaning skillfully, but they are also norms that dictate how women are to comport themselves. Akerman is flouting both. She explains that she cast herself in the main role because of her ineptitude at being feminine. She says, "I am a female Charlie Chaplin, I could have made slapstick comedy . . . My body in a movie is very important, it says something by itself, it has the weight of the Real."[44] As Akerman said in an interview, in her childhood she grew painfully aware of her clumsiness. She started to think that "the other girls were already built to fit what a young woman was raised to become, in conformity with their future as women in a normative society."[45] She is alluding to the process of socialization that Beauvoir outlines, the long and arduous path from "girl" to "woman." By casting herself in the main role in this film, Akerman is in a sense contributing to "denaturalizing" housework by subverting the assumption that girls are naturally fit to do it.[46]

In the shoe polish scene, Akerman is seated on the floor, surrounded by pots and pans. At first, she seems to be trying to polish her shoes with black polish, only accidentally running the brush across her socks. Of course, we have reasons to doubt her intentions from the start since someone who really wanted to polish their shoes would have taken them off. She begins smearing polish over her socks all the way up her calves. She is doing this with great gusto (Figure 12).

Akerman is not accidentally failing at the task, but deliberately doing a bad job. Is she too impatient to do it well? Is it that she cannot be bothered? Or has she decided that she would prefer to have shoeshine smeared skin, maybe because it would annoy her mother? These are the sorts of questions we might ask ourselves while watching her behavior. The film itself does not provide any hint of her train of thought during this sequence or, for that matter, during any other.[47]

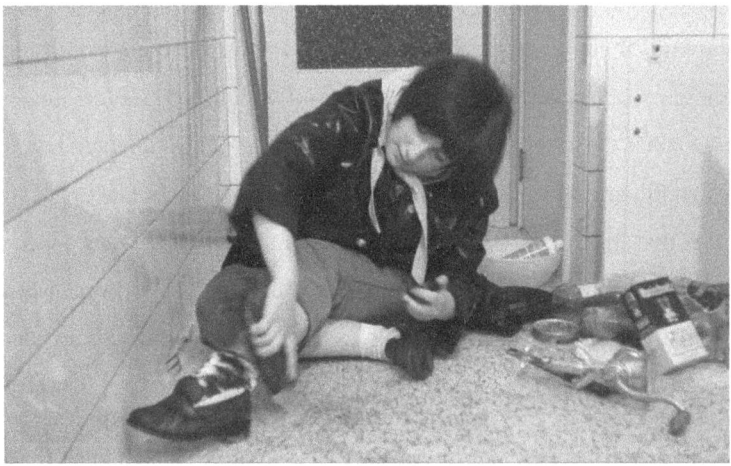

FIGURE 12 Blow Up My Town *directed by Chantal Akerman 1968. Collections CINEMATEK—© Fondation Chantal Akerman.*

In *Jeanne Dielman*, Jeanne starts her mornings by polishing her son's shoes before he gets out of bed.⁴⁸ Jeanne will also mess it up the second time; the brush will fly out of her hand. But she won't mess up in the way in which Akerman here does. Jeanne's movements are decisive, effective, and controlled. Akerman's are exaggeratedly graceless.

*Blow Up My Town* is Akerman's overt homage to Godard's *Pierrot Le Fou*, which she often cites as the film that made her decide to become a director. *Pierrot Le Fou* is about a husband and father who runs away from his bourgeois life, hits the road with a free-spirited woman, and eventually blows himself up. Indeed, *Blow Up My Town* is peppered with allusions to Godard, from the smeared skin to the explosive ending, and pervaded by a similar sense of mischief and havoc. But *Blow Up My Town* is arguably less optimistic than the film that inspired it. While Pierrot changes his mind in the end about blowing himself up and struggles in vain to extinguish the flame he has lit, Akerman shows no hesitation to self-destruct when she tapes shut the cracks in the door and windows and turns on the gas. Pierrot's death is also staged in nature with a view of the open sea.⁴⁹ Akerman is confined to a claustrophobic space, "her town" a desolate urban landscape, a generic apartment building, and even more narrowly, the kitchen. In the world of *Blow Up My Town*, there seem to be only two options available to a teenager like Akerman: either submit to the demands of the kitchen or blow it all up.

## Images between Images

Six years later, Akerman directed *Jeanne Dielman, 23, quai du Commerce, 1080 Bruxelles* (1975), which was hailed as a masterpiece as soon as it was released. The film covers three consecutive days in the life of a bourgeois housewife named Jeanne Dielman, a widow who lives with Sylvain, her teenage son, at the address cited in the full title. Although it is famous for its absence of action, it is also a film brimming with activity. We follow Jeanne's restless movements from room to room, from store to store as she searches for a missing button, down the street, and up the elevator. One way to summarize the film would be to say that it makes the work that it takes to establish and maintain domestic order, which was merely implied in *Blow Up My Town*, its focus. Here are some of her household chores: Jeanne picks up her son's clothes for the day, serves him breakfast, makes his bed and hers, cleans the dishes in the sink, lights the stove, tidies the living room, dusts the shelves, runs errands at the grocer's and the butcher's, eats a sandwich in the kitchen, watches her neighbor's baby, peels potatoes, kneads a meatloaf, and knits a sweater. As Zara Joan Miller has put it, "The monotony of housework, a repetition Simone de Beauvoir likened to Sisyphean torture, is given center stage in Akerman's film."[50] The film's duration (three hours and twenty-one minutes) allows us to track this structure across time and to see the ways in which Jeanne's activities repeat themselves with only minor variations from one day to the next. We are shown two complete 24-hour cycles that include repetitions: Jeanne polishes her son's shoes twice, makes coffee and breakfast twice, washes dishes and dries cutlery twice, and turns her son's bed back into a sofa twice.[51]

We also learn very early in the film that Jeanne works as a prostitute who is visited by different johns at the same hour in the late afternoons. It is a significant fact that these visits last exactly as long as it takes to boil the potatoes.[52] Jeanne's clients "are slotted into the housewife's timetable alongside other chores, apparently sharing the same status in her routines as more mundane tasks in her regulated work pattern."[53] When the john arrives, the viewer is left behind in a darkening hallway, the dimming light indicating the passage of time. It is only in the penultimate scene that we are allowed to follow Jeanne into the bedroom.[54] This is also the scene of the film's sole cinematic "event," with Jeanne stabbing her client in the neck with a pair of scissors. The ending was criticized at the time of the film's release as a concession to traditional narrative, even though this dramatic event is treated no differently from anything else that takes place in the film.[55]

Prior to this "climax," we see each john pay and leave, at which point Jeanne throws her earnings into a soup tureen placed prominently on the dining room table. This soup tureen is also where she goes to pick up cash for groceries. The association we are invited to make is that she is supporting herself and her son not only through her housework, but also through her sex work, which earns her a wage. Jeanne's prostitution has been a point of interest in feminist readings of this film. Akerman herself called it a "metaphor," perhaps for Jeanne's social situation at large: even though Jeanne is a widow and so does not need to perform what Beauvoir calls "bed service" as a part of the marital contract, she still has to do the "work" of sex in order to be able to support herself.[56] In essays such as "Why Sexuality Is Work," Federici includes sex as part of housework in a broader sense, because it becomes one of the many tasks that women are expected to perform in order to service workers, ordinarily without pay.

The year before *Jeanne Dielman* was released, Laura Mulvey published her seminal essay, "Visual Pleasure and Narrative Cinema," in which she introduced the concept of the "male gaze" and revealed its workings in Hollywood films, taking Hitchcock's *Vertigo* as the paradigm.[57] According to Mulvey, mainstream movies cast women on screen "as erotic object for the characters within the screen story, and as erotic object for the spectator within the auditorium."[58] She describes this dynamic in terms of a voyeuristic visual pleasure made possible by identifying with the male lead in the film and assuming his objectifying look. Although Mulvey was not yet familiar with Akerman when she wrote the essay, she later claimed that *Jeanne Dielman* had "turned cinema upside down."[59] Unlike the films that Mulvey was describing, *Jeanne Dielman* is composed of extended shots without reverse shots or close-ups. Akerman once again positioned the camera at her own short height and claimed that it was important to her that the viewer know exactly where she was standing in relation to Jeanne. She did not want to spy on Jeanne. We are supposed to know, and presumably Jeanne is supposed to know, where the camera is located and what it can witness.

In an early shot, Akerman even ended up cutting off the top of Jeanne's head. Jeanne is at the door welcoming a john. All we are shown is the middle part of her body, with her arms folded in front (Figure 13). The impression is quite different from the similarly headless shot in *D'Est*, where the image calls to mind violence done to human bodies. It is also quite different from another instance of visual dissection, the opening sequence of Godard's *Contempt*. Brigitte Bardot is lying naked in bed while the male character is describing parts of her body and the camera is gliding down her figure. It is no surprise that *Jeanne Dielman* came to be seen as an answer to the demands of feminist film criticism.[60] Akerman had resisted the illusion of a privileged point of view, excluded a male lead whose

FIGURE 13 Jeanne Dielman 23, quai du Commerce, 1080 Bruxelles directed by Chantal Akerman 1975. Collections CINEMATEK— © Fondation Chantal Akerman.

perspective we could be invited to occupy, and thwarted a voyeuristic pleasure of the male-gaze variety. As she puts it, "You know it wasn't shot through the keyhole."[61] Although we watch so much of what Jeanne does, we remain at a respectful distance. We are once again giving a character the space to lead their own real life, of which we see only a curated segment.

Akerman had high ambitions for the film. Although it cannot be said to have a political agenda comparable to the Wages for Housework campaign, it does seek to open a new perspective and bring housework out of the shadows to which it has been relegated. According to Akerman: "I made this film to give all these actions that are typically devalued a life on film."[62] On the one hand, Akerman is responding to the fact that housework is devalued in life, that it tends to be taken for granted by those who benefit from it. On the other hand, Akerman was also responding more specifically to the devaluation of housework in film. This led to her decision to make a film that consists almost entirely of what she calls the "images between images," those images that end up on the cutting room floor if they even make it onto the reel. As Akerman explains, she wanted to invert the "hierarchy of images" that has shaped conventional representations of women. Akerman inverts this hierarchy by "showing cooking and hiding sex."[63] Her film has the more specific aim of changing our sense of what is worth watching.

As Akerman tells it, her decision to cast a glamorous movie star in the role of Jeanne was in the service of making housework, in a literal sense, visible to people who are used to taking it for granted. Akerman met Delphine Seyrig at a film festival where she was promoting *Hotel Monterey*. She was immediately struck by Seyrig as a "magnificent platinum blonde" and she even wrote the script for *Jeanne Dielman* with Seyrig in mind. What made her ideal for the part, according to Akerman, is her divergence from the character of Jeanne. Seyrig did not give the impression that housework was second nature to her. Although she is not a magnificent platinum blonde in the film, Seyrig's version of Jeanne can have an alienation effect on the viewer, remaining always a little bit out of visual sync from the character we are asked to picture. The director Danièle Huillet was annoyed. She complained that Seyrig looks like she has never peeled potatoes in her life.[64] But Akerman explains that "if we saw someone making beds and doing dishes whom we normally see doing those things, we wouldn't really see that person. Just like the men who are blind to their wives doing dishes. So it had to be someone we didn't usually see do the dishes. So, Delphine was perfect because it suddenly became visible."[65] Akerman makes clear that she was not interested in showing housework as it is done by the legions of women who do it every day and who do not look like Seyrig. Her aim was never a realistic (or *veristic*) depiction of housework, or of housewives.

As Ivone Margulies has argued, *Jeanne Dielman* is a "hyperrealist" film because the reality it shows is mediated, informed by the filmed image. To this end, Akerman wanted a Jeanne who would have been recognizable to her audience as a movie star, someone that has already appeared on screen. It is also striking that she picked a movie star known for her feminist politics. For example, a year after *Jeanne Dielman,* Seyrig was involved in making a video of herself reading excerpts of Valerie Solanas's *SCUM Manifesto* out of print in France at the time, while Carole Roussopoulos types out its words.

But Akerman walks a fine line. On the one hand, it would be fair to say that she tries to represent housework faithfully, truthfully. She thinks that what is needed in order to do so is to represent it lovingly, motivated by a love for the work itself. On the other hand, Akerman deliberately abstracts away from many aspects of housework as it is actually performed. She illuminates some aspects of housework while leaving others eclipsed. As she put it, she wanted to draw attention to the *daily gestures* of a woman. She did not say that she wanted to draw attention to the women who perform these daily gestures. So, casting Seyrig was a means to an end. We are to notice not her, but what it is that she does: her making of beds, her doing of dishes.

## Conscious Housework

That said, Akerman is interested in the woman who performs housework in a specific sense, because she is interested in what this woman reveals and does not reveal. A case in point is the second day, when Jeanne's regimented routine begins to unravel. We are not shown what it is that happened, though we are led to assume that it happened behind closed doors, while Jeanne was meeting one of her johns. The film is careful to avoid an easy explanation—all it presents to us is the aftermath of the unseen event. Her hair is a mess, she forgets to place the lid on the soup tureen, lets the potatoes cook for too long, and runs aimlessly from room to room without being able to decide what to do with the overcooked potatoes.

Akerman herself did eventually provide an explanation. She said that Jeanne has the first orgasm of her life during the second john's visit. This orgasm was supposedly her undoing, maybe because there was no room for sexual pleasure in her life, or maybe because the absence of pleasure in heterosexual sex was a source of her freedom from men.[66] Akerman goes on to clarify that during the third visit Jeanne experiences the second orgasm of her life, and this orgasm propels her to stab her client. But Jeanne's expressions during the one sex scene we do see are equivocal at best. They also suggest disgust and repulsion.[67] Given that the film does not show the first orgasm and leaves the second orgasm up for debate, we are not compelled to accept Akerman's explanation. The interpretation I favor is that Jeanne experiences a moment of unbidden reflection, a "thought of being" totally unprovoked by anything that happens, and it is this thought that throws her routine forever out of whack.[68]

Be that as it may, Jeanne Dielman as a person is undeniably uncanny. While she cuts a familiar figure, her gestures are also too repetitive, too inflexible, too immanent. Jeanne's routine even exceeds the chores that are strictly speaking necessary for maintaining domestic order, for it encompasses even pastimes such as visiting the neighborhood café, listening to the radio, and taking a walk with her son around the block after dinner. Jeanne has turned every activity, whether or not it belongs to housework proper, into a routine. As Akerman has often stressed, Jeanne has developed a highly specific relationship to time by structuring each day in such a way as to exclude a single vacant moment. Everything that Jeanne does has been settled in advance, inserted into its exact place in her daily schedule. What is motivating her to devote her days so fully to these chores? And what is it that she is thinking about while doing them? She herself does not tell us. The dialogue is kept to a bare minimum and is delivered in a monotonous tone, a mark of the anti-naturalist acting style that Akerman preferred. In effect, whatever Jeanne does express, she expresses through her body, her pace, her comportment in space. It is difficult to watch Jeanne's relentless busyness and not wonder what it is that is moving her to take the next step.[69]

Jeanne's inner life has inspired much commentary. Sometimes Jeanne is described as someone suffering from obsessive-compulsive disorder, which would disqualify her as an exemplar of the bourgeois housewife as such. Most often Jeanne has been described as robotic. Irene Corpas calls her a "mechanical body" and "an engine that does not stop."[70] In Jayne Loader's words, Jeanne "is presented as an automaton, geared for maximum efficiency and functioning perfectly."[71] In a slightly different vein, Stanley Cavell has suggested that Jeanne does not have a sense of self that could be recounted in the form of a story, because such a sense would require the ability to distinguish what matters from what does not, and the film denies her this ability by placing all events on the same level. As Cavell puts it, *Jeanne Dielman* is a "study, or materialization, of the self as a collection, in the particular form in which the one who is subject of the collection is not free (or not moved?) to supply a narrative."[72] By contrast, Salomé Aguilera Skvirsky argues that "[i]n *Jeanne Dielman* the invisible housewife (as a role) gains visibility not *despite* her household labor or apart from it, but *through* it. The character's personhood is expressed *in* her work, *not* in her leisure: she is what she does."[73] These readings raise a bigger question of whether we are being asked to see Jeanne as a conscious being with any inner life. Is Jeanne the kind of subject who has lived experiences and so is even capable of frustration with housework's endless repetitions?

In a "making-of" documentary, *Autour de Jeanne Dielman*, the young Akerman gives the more mature Seyrig the explicit instruction not to "psychologize" the character, not even through subtle facial expressions.[74] Although Seyrig is as opposed to psychologizing as Akerman, she wants to be able to contribute something to Jeanne, even if only "internally." For example, the two of them have an extensive exchange about Jeanne brushing her hair. Akerman insists that Seyrig is to perform the gesture slowly. Seyrig would like to know why, what is going through Jeanne's mind, whether she is daydreaming. Akerman seems to think that Jeanne's visible behavior should answer this question; as she points out, Jeanne closed the door in order to brush her hair. Seyrig reminds Akerman that even this gesture is ambiguous—she could have closed the door for many reasons. Although Akerman hesitates to put it into words, she eventually expresses it in the following way: "She's not daydreaming, it's a moment of relaxation for herself." Seyrig is appeased, adding that this is what she meant by daydreaming, that she's relaxing. As their exchange makes clear, whether Jeanne is daydreaming depends on what is meant by daydreaming, how much structure is built into this activity. Is Jeanne thinking about something, or nothing? But Akerman and Seyrig are on the same page in one respect. Neither seems to entertain the possibility that Jeanne could be a mere machine geared for maximum efficiency.

So, Akerman's refusal to include facial expressions that correspond to states of mind does not mean that Jeanne is supposed to be an outer shell or empty husk. In another impressive feat of abstraction, Akerman succeeds in setting psychology aside only to make Jeanne's consciousness all the more salient. Consider the sequence during which Jeanne is drinking a cup of coffee in the kitchen. She pours herself a cup, followed by milk, taking a sip. Her face suggests displeasure. Her eyes descend to the cup, the culprit. She hurries over to the sink to pour it out. She gets another glass, smells the milk, and pours it into the second glass. This taste seems fine, for she pours herself another cup of coffee from the thermos, followed by milk, this time adding two cubes of sugar, which she compares by placing them side by side on the table. After stirring the coffee for a while, she takes another sip, and her eyes descend toward the cup again (Figure 14). The coffee is unsalvageable; she will have to brew a new batch. Through a series of gestures, specifically through the direction of her gaze, we watch her train of thought. This is hardly the image of a mechanical body. Although Akerman claims to be more interested in "results" than in "motives," she is repeatedly gesturing at what lies behind Jeanne's subtle shifts in expression.

Akerman describes the process of writing the script as quick and easy, since most of what she was putting on the page was already in her "blood."[75] Similar to Federici's childhood memories, Akerman only

FIGURE 14 Jeanne Dielman 23, quai du Commerce, 1080 Bruxelles directed by Chantal Akerman 1975. Collections CINEMATEK— © Fondation Chantal Akerman.

needed to recall watching the women in her family while growing up. As she puts it, for them, "everything had to be turned into a ritual in a way to replace Jewish ritual. Because in Jewish ritual practically every activity of the day is ritualized."[76] She is referring to the fading of ritual from one generation to the next, but also to the vanishing of an Eastern European way of life.[77] During the documentary, Babette Mangolte even exclaims, "That's Jeanne Dielman—a Polish Jew!" Although Jeanne's biography is kept to a bare minimum in the film, her resemblance to Nelly makes its way into one of Jeanne's late-night conversations with her son, during which she mentions that her parents were dead by the end of the war. Such details help make Jeanne into an individual with a backstory rather than casting her as a mere product of social pressures to enact a generic role. They also shed light on the relationship that Jeanne develops toward her domestic chores. What they suggest is that regimenting one's day into a series of rituals is perhaps a way of coping with trauma. Despite Akerman's refusal to psychologize the character, she claimed that Jeanne's routine is in the service of "holding her life together" and "keeping anxiety at bay."[78] This would make Jeanne's housework negatively motivated, driven by avoidance of something she would prefer not to confront. Even though Jeanne is not primarily battling Beauvoir's indefeasible enemies of dirt, dust, and decay, she is fighting against a standing threat that could unravel her life.

But this way of putting it can be misleading. I am also struck by the extent to which Jeanne seems to derive positive satisfaction from housework not often acknowledged. On the first day, many of her gestures are easy, calm, and smooth. She glides, even saunters, from room to room, clearly enjoying the calibrated choreography of her routine. She takes pride in the work, especially in the details that she accomplishes with great precision, for example, ensuring that the veal cutlets have been folded just right on the plate. We even catch glimpses of ordinary pleasures that break into her day. There is the tactile quality of handling the meat, smoothing the bed covers, and folding the clothes. Then there are the moments of repose that her routine affords: drinking a cup of coffee with her feet lazily crossed, taking the time to brush her hair, and relishing a perfectly boiled potato. Jeanne does not seem to be secretly yearning for an open future in Beauvoir's sense. When she finds herself with nothing to do, she looks distraught, desperate. This comes to a head on the third day when she gets up an hour earlier than usual and is faced with the prospect of unstructured time. We can feel Jeanne's mounting anxiety. She tries to busy herself with the neighbor's baby, making it scream every time she lifts it from its carrycot. She sits in her armchair, her hands almost clutching its armrests in a state of unease. Finishing her work early does not yield Beauvoir's pleasure of contemplation. What appears to give her pleasure is the work itself, or its ephemeral achievements.[79]

Jeanne's efforts to keep anxiety at bay can only be effective if what she is doing is able to hold her attention and engage her mind. If we accept Beauvoir's identification of immanence and mechanism, we are led to assume that doing housework involves repeating a series of gestures mechanically in the sense of thoughtlessly. This is in part what is supposed to make it so dissatisfying to a conscious being. But the seamlessness of Jeanne's routine on the first day shows that her attention is ordinarily occupied by her work. It is also given direction by this work, for the task at hand dictates what to notice and what to ignore. When it comes to certain kinds of household chores, such as washing dishes, these might be perfect opportunities to let your mind roam. When taken as a whole, housework is indeed cognitively demanding. Usually, we see her eyes fixed and focused on whatever it is that she is doing in the moment. But Jeanne is also seemingly thinking about what it is that she needs to do *next*: drying the cutlery, breading the veal cutlets, knitting the sweater. Jeanne needs to keep track of the task that awaits her if she is to proceed in a specific order, to turn on and off the lights in every room, to remove all traces of the johns before her son returns from school. Of course, the very fact that housework occupies the mind does not necessarily make it a source of satisfaction. A person unlike Jeanne might find the mental exertion of housework to be one of its torments. Jeanne does not want to be thinking about anything other than what she is doing.

Jeanne's unraveling illuminates the sophistication of her routine, for it is by considering what has gone badly that we discover what it takes for it to go well. On the second day, she performs many of the same activities, for the most part in the right order, but with evident mistakes: she drops the brush while polishing her son's shoes, she drops a spoon while drying the cutlery. As viewers, we might not have noticed the extent to which Jeanne is mentally present until the moment in the film when Jeanne's "inner life detaches from her activity."[80] After the second john's visit, Jeanne is visibly distracted. She forgets to put the lid back onto the soup tureen or to turn on the light in the bathroom. She flits aimlessly from room to room. The potato peeling scene is a case in point. Once she overcooks the potatoes, throws them out, and purchases new ones, she seats herself at the kitchen table ready to peel a new batch. She is running low on time (her son is about to return) and yet she is peeling them absent-

FIGURE 15 Jeanne Dielman 23, quai du Commerce, 1080 Bruxelles directed by Chantal Akerman 1975. Collections CINEMATEK— © Fondation Chantal Akerman

mindedly and unskillfully (Figure 15). She runs her knife over the already peeled areas as if she were only barely aware of which part still needs to be peeled. At one point, she pulls herself together and picks up speed. Now she attacks the potato like an unpleasant chore. Whatever it is to which her thoughts are being drawn—and at this point we no longer know what—it is evidently taking her away from the present moment. And in those rare scenes of rest, moments like those in the elevator when Jeanne is not doing anything, her mind is elsewhere. The film is so masterful in showing this presence and absence of attention, and the way in which housework, when done skillfully, does engage her mind.[81]

Akerman described *Blow Up My Town* and *Jeanne Dielman* as love letters to her mother. In *Jeanne Dielman* in particular, she thought that she was honoring the work done by her mother and other women in her family by depicting their daily gestures as precisely as she could. But this does not mean that it is a love letter to the work itself. Akerman came to recognize in hindsight that her film is not exactly a celebration of the lives that her mother and aunts led, lives structured according to the rhythms of housework. Like Beauvoir, Akerman couldn't shake her sense that Jeanne's world is suffocatingly small, limited to her apartment on *quai du Commerce*, a world of "confinement" and of "repetition."[82] She later described *Jeanne Dielman* as "a kind of mirror that wasn't necessarily something [the women in her family] appreciated seeing," and she wondered whether it was kind of her to throw this mirror in her mother's face. As she puts it, "I thought for a while that I was speaking on [my mother's] behalf, and then sometimes I'd think, I was speaking against her."[83] Here she echoes what she said with respect to Nelly's traumatic experiences, that she came to realize that it is not appropriate for her to speak in her mother's stead. She now adds her suspicion that such an attentive depiction of her mother's life was a form of betrayal.[84] She seems to be grappling with a set of difficulties that Beauvoir and Federici also faced when dealing with their mothers' lives. How do you represent housework without idealizing it or dismissing it, and by implication, the women who do it? And how do you make the significance of housework visible to those who tend to take it for granted while at the same time raising the "heads," "consciousness," "gaze" of those who have been expected to bear its burden?

Housework makes Jeanne's life meaningful to her because it provides order and structure, because it calls for skillfully directed attention, and because it includes opportunities for care, ease, and pleasure. In contrast to Federici's emphasis on housework's social value, Akerman explores its personal value, what might motivate someone to perform it beyond the more obvious pressure to do so. Though Federici and Akerman share some of Beauvoir's concerns about lives devoted to housework, they are more explicitly invested in making housework *visible* and illuminating its significance. Their aim is to foreground the patterns of which housework is comprised, both from the inside (the one doing it) and the outside (the one evaluating it). This would make *Jeanne Dielman* a qualified antidote to Beauvoir's grim vision of housework. Akerman is also doing more than offering a counterexample, for she is exposing the neglected significance that housework can have for those whose lives are devoted to it. It might be relatively easy to reject it as dissatisfying from the perspective of the daughter who wants to avoid her mother's fate, though this is less straightforward for those who do this work on a daily basis. But as

Akerman herself insists, "It's not a film with a message," so she is not defending a thesis that could be compared to Beauvoir's and Federici's.[85] According to Akerman's own intentions, which were not always honored, this is a film not about women or housewives in general, but about a very specific woman in a very specific situation.

*Jeanne Dielman* moreover focuses on the stark divide between what we can and cannot know about its central character. In *Autour de Jeanne Dielman*, Seyrig asks Akerman in exasperation, "How can I play her if I don't know her secrets?" Akerman knew that some secrets cannot or should not be disclosed. *Jeanne Dielman* ends with arguably the most enigmatic image in the entire film, a shot not of Jeanne stabbing her client, but of Jeanne sitting nearly motionless at her dining room table, cloaked in the semi-darkness of the late afternoon. There is blood on her cream blouse and on her hand. Her elbows are leaning against the reflective surface of the table, which throws back at us a mirror image of her bloody blouse and hand. We stay with her for seven minutes in this state of repose, watching her face, which seems to have gone slack. It is the first time she is at rest, or the first time she seems to embrace rest without anxiety. It is almost a post-nut clarity after the true climax of the film, not the orgasm but the killing. As Akerman insists, it is not possible to know what Jeanne is thinking. As she put it in an interview with Gary Indiana, "[Y]ou don't understand her. You never will. I hope you never will—that's the strength of the film."

Several decades later, Akerman made an installation based on this final shot. It consists of seven screens with a time lapse, all showing Jeanne in her state of repose at the dining room table. Akerman titled the installation "Woman Sitting after Killing." It alludes to what happened just before this scene, and it abstracts away from Jeanne's individuality, turning her into a woman in general.[86] Because the screens are slightly out of sync, we begin to notice a variety of postures and gestures. It turns out that Jeanne is not motionless. She sighs, she blinks, she relaxes her shoulders, she lowers her head and then lifts it and tilts it. At one point, a smile appears to flicker across her face. The installation highlights that Jeanne is not a mere surface that repels our assumptions or projections. There is something going on inside her, we just don't have direct access to it. In that same interview with Gary Indiana, Akerman continues: "You will never know what is happening in her mind and in her heart. I don't know either... It's not Jeanne Dielman's secret, it's Delphine's secret."[87] Seyrig may have been frustrated that Akerman never told her Jeanne's secret. Here Akerman is saying that Seyrig did know it, because it is also her secret, the secret that she brings to the table. By respecting Jeanne's privacy, Akerman in fact cleared space for Seyrig's own "internal" contribution, making the character of Jeanne the fruit of a genuine collaboration.[88]

# Notes

1 Amy Taubin, https://www.artforum.com/columns/from-the-archives-amy-taubin-on-chantal-akermans-jeanne-dielman-190095/. Taubin regrets giving the film a negative review when it first came out: "I ascribe my blindness and misreading to my identification of Jeanne with my own mother and my inability to reconcile the character's final horrific but life-changing act with anything my mother would do. I apologize. Jeanne Dielman is the mother of us all."

2 For the significance of this sound of gas, see Schmid, *Chantal Akerman*, p. 50.

3 Criterion Channel interview.

4 In Virginie Despentes's new novel, *Dear Dickhead*, an aging actress complains about a part: "There are scenes of me in the kitchen, cooking. I don't make movies so people can film me doing the dishes" (p. 117).

5 "When it came out, *Jeanne Dielman* was fully in tune with the European women's movement—'Peeling Potatoes' was one of the articles in an issue of *Les temps modernes* edited by Simone de Beauvoir." Ivone Margulies, "A Matter of Time" (https://www.criterion.com/current/posts/1215-a-matter-of-time-jeanne-dielman-23-quai-du-commerce-1080-bruxelles). For a fuller discussion of Jeanne Dielman in this historical context, see also Ivone Margulies, *Nothing Happens*, pp. 140–8.

6 https://americanart.si.edu/artwork/semiotics-kitchen-77211.

7 For a comparison between the two, see https://screenqueens.wordpress.com/2018/09/29/objects-and-domesticity-in-jeanne-dielman-and-semiotics-of-the-kitchen/. Also, Roos van der Lint claims, "*Semiotics of the Kitchen* . . . is unmistakably indebted to Akerman's first film [*Blow Up My Town*]. Irrespective of whether the influence was direct or indirect, what is certain is that feminism was in the air, and Akerman led the way with this theme" (*Chantal Akerman: Passages*, p. 94).

8 Margulies's has argued that in *Jeanne Dielman*, Akerman was not interested in featuring representatives of identity groups. She contrasts it with films made by Yvonne Rainer, who calls her characters "she" and "he" in order to underscore that they are generic types.

9 Quoted in Bergstrom, "Invented Memories," p. 107.

10 In *A Family in Brussels*, a character similar to Jeanne Dielman is described in the following way: "She's very good at not letting herself think about what she doesn't want to think about, at least she is trying to be good at it. She is trying and it's so tiring" (p. 9).

11 Quoted in "Angela Martin: Chantal Akerman on Jeanne Dielman. Excerpts from an Interview with Camera Obscura, November 1976," in: Camera Obscura 2 (1977), pp. 118–19. During the interview at BAMPFA, Akerman added: "the fact that I wanted to show those gestures as precisely as I could . . . If you do that it is because you love them. In some way you recognize those gestures. They were always denied and ignored."

12 https://www.moussemagazine.it/magazine/chantal-akerman-elisabeth-lebovici-2011/.

13 Beauvoir, *The Second Sex*, p. 474.

14 Ibid., p. 7.

15 The reference to Sisyphus is an allusion to her former friend Camus's famous version of the ancient myth. According to Camus, the gods punished Sisyphus by making him push the same rock up a hill over and over again, because they "thought with some reason" (in Camus's words) "that there is no more dreadful punishment than futile and hopeless labor." But there is a difference between Camus's and Beauvoir's uses of this myth. For Camus, Sisyphus's predicament seems to represent the human condition. For Beauvoir, it is only activities that have a structure similar to housework.

16 Beauvoir, *The Second Sex*, p. 470.

17 Ibid., p. 474.

18 Beauvoir mentions women, who let preserves go moldy in order to try to "preserve" them, as evidence that housewives are trying to create lasting achievements.

19 Beauvoir: "[D]ay after day it repeats itself in identical form from century to century; it produces nothing new" (*The Second Sex* p. 73).

20 This does not imply that cooking just needs to become appreciated by husbands and children, in which case it can be made into a transcendent project.

21 Susan Okin (in *Justice, Gender, and the Family*) has provided a similar critique of marriage, according to which the gendered division of labor within marriages is one of its central problems. See especially pp. 149–55.

22 As Andrea Veltman argues ("The Sisyphean Torture of Housework"), Beauvoir's criticism of housework is integral to her criticism of marriage as an institution.

23 She discusses this more extensively in her *Ethics of Ambiguity*.

24 Beauvoir, *A Very Easy Death*, p. 36.

25 Ibid., p. 43.

26 Ibid., p. 35.

27 By taking the bourgeois housewife as her paradigm case, she was neglecting and sometimes even distorting the experiences of working-class women and women of color.

28 Katrina Forrester ("Feminist Demands and the Problem of Housework") argues that demand-making practices should be evaluated in terms of disclosing social conditions and setting revolutionary political horizons that exceed the content of those demands. She also claims that the Wages for Housework campaign developed a "distinctive vision of what demand-making can accomplish" (p. 1281).

29 Federici also insisted that material conditions need to change, and she expressed skepticism about the political potential of consciousness-raising on its own: "One of the main shortcomings of the women's movement has been its tendency to overemphasize the role of consciousness in the context of social change, as if enslavement were a mental condition and liberation could be achieved by an act of will" (*Revolution Point Zero*, pp. 55–6).

30 As Federici puts it, "It is important to recognize that when we speak of housework we are not speaking of a job like other jobs, but we are speaking of the most pervasive manipulation, and the subtlest violence that capitalism has ever perpetrated against any section of the working class" (p. 16).

31 Other examples would be labor under the conditions of slavery, colonialism, prisons, and so on.

32 Federici, *Revolution Point Zero*, p. 31.

33 As Carmen Teeple Hopkins argues ("Mostly Work, Little Play"), women of color who work as live-in domestic help are especially vulnerable to exploitation, since the boundary between their paid work time and their unpaid personal time tends to become completely erased.

34 Housework will vary based on expectations of cleanliness and of professional appearance and behavior.

35 Federici, *Revolution Point Zero*, p. 2.

36 Federici also acknowledged that many women want to continue performing housework and that the feminist movement needs to be sensitive to their situation. See pp. 56–7.

37 Ibid., p. 19.

38 Ibid., p. 1.

39 Ibid., p. 15.

40 Ibid., p. 2.

41  Skvirsky notes that the "town" in the title alludes to community and tradition that are never explicitly shown but that provide the broader context in which her activities take place (*The Process Genre*, p. 125).

42  Smurfs are Belgian, so it locates the film in a national context.

43  Marion Schmid, *Chantal Akerman*, p. 19.

44  https://www.moussemagazine.it/magazine/chantal-akerman-elisabeth-lebovici-2011/.

45  Ibid.

46  This is a suggestion that Kate Rennebohm makes on the podcast "The Akerman Year."

47  Schmid suggests a psychological reading, which is that Akerman's character is suffering from heartbreak, an inner disturbance, and a psychic implosion (see pp. 18–19). I am generally unsympathetic to such readings of Akerman's film, of which there are many examples.

48  Akerman even brings these two scenes together, juxtaposing them in the montage she made for her self-portrait *Chantal Akerman by Chantal Akerman*.

49  For a more extensive contrast between the French New Wave and Akerman, see Irene Valle Corpas, "Between Home and Flight."

50  Zara Joan Miller, "Repetition and Insistence in Akerman and Bausch," p. 122.

51  There are also explicit references to the routine in the film. For example, Jeanne tells her neighbor what it is that she cooks every Tuesday. The film has often been described as taking place in "real time," which Akerman has strongly denied. How could it be taking place in real time since it covers three days but doesn't last three days? Instead, Akerman is showing the actual duration of specific activities like peeling potatoes, though she often relies on editing.

52  Potatoes play a large role in this film. This might have been for personal reasons. In *My Mother Laughs* Akerman recounts that the only story about her time in Auschwitz her mother was willing to tell was that her friend saved her life by stealing potatoes.

53  Schmid, *Chantal Akerman*, p. 35.

54  This makes *Jeanne Dielman* importantly different from films such as Lizzie Borden's *Working Girls* (1986), which focus on the conditions of sex work rather than on housework.

55  Marguerite Duras was very critical of the ending. Stanley Cavell as well.

56  See Lori Marso, "Perverse Protests." In an interview from 1976 with Kate Horsefield and Lyn Blumenthal, Akerman said that she wanted to compare marriage and prostitution.

57  In a twist of fate, *Vertigo* was demoted to second place in the recent *Sight and Sound* poll, in which *Jeanne Dielman* rose to the top.

58  Laura Mulvey, "Visual Pleasure and Narrative Cinema," p. 809.

59  She calls for an alternative cinema that responds critically to "these obsessions and assumptions" that preface Hollywood productions but claims that "it can still only exist as a counterpoint" (Mulvey, "Visual Pleasure and Narrative Cinema," p. 805). This is true of Akerman as well. Although Akerman is breaking so many rules, she understands what she is doing in critical response to the mainstream. It suggests that she is inextricably bound to that which she is criticizing.

60  See, for example, Annette Kuhn, *Women's Pictures*, p. 169.

61  Quoted in Schmid, *Chantal Akerman*, p. 48.

62  Criterion Channel interview.

63  Margulies, "A Matter of Time."

64  Helge Heberle and Monika Funke Stern, "Das Feuer im Stern des Berges," p. 11. Huillet also complains that Akerman was too strict with her camera by allowing Jeanne's head to be cut off.

65  Criterion Channel interview.

66  Akerman claims that not having had an orgasm is what held Jeanne's life together.

67  Brenda Longfellow:

> In a random survey of women friends who had seen the film, the readings seem to divide, interestingly enough, according to the sexual preference of the spectator. For the lesbian spectator, Jeanne's response represents a flash of consciousness and a frightening recognition of her own alienation, her own status as sexual object. For the heterosexual female spectator, the movement of the head and arm connote sexual

pleasure, an eruption of the disordering possibility of desire against which Jeanne reacts with a gesture of violent negation. ("Love Letters to the Mother" p. 84)

68  This is a possibility that interested Hubert Dreyfus:

> As second baseman for the New York Yankees, Knoblauch was... voted best infielder of the year, but one day, rather than simply fielding a hit and throwing the ball to first base, it seems he stepped back and took up a "free, distanced orientation" towards the ball and how he was throwing it—the mechanics of it, as he put it. After that, he couldn't recover his former absorption and often—though not always—threw the ball to first base erratically—once into the face of a spectator. ("Return of the Myth of the Mental," p. 354)

69  In 1983, Akerman made a documentary about Pina Bausch (*One Day Pina Asked...*) and expressed an affinity with her dance performances, which were also focused on repetitive movements. As Miller puts it, for both Akerman and Bausch, "[i]t is not so much an attempt to free the hamster but to understand its relationship to its wheel" ("Repetition and Insistence: Akerman and Bausch," p. 121). Akerman captures her ambivalence toward this type of repetitive structure when in her documentary she says that at first Bausch's performances gave her something close to happiness, but then she developed a resistance to them, and even had to close her eyes.

70  Irene Corpas, "Between Flight and Home," p. 4.

71  Jayne Loader, "Jeanne Dielman: Death in Installments."

72  Cavell, *Here and There*, p. 48. According to Cavell, Akerman's film shows that women are especially affected by what he calls the "violence of the ordinary" which erases any difference between what matters and what does not.

73  Skvirsky, *Process Genre*, p. 206.

74  The footage was filmed by Sami Frey and later edited by Akerman and Agnes Ravez. In the documentary, Seyrig wants to smile while reading Jeanne's sister's letter out loud. But Akerman wants the letter read in a rhythmic, liturgic tone. In *Nothing Happens,* Margulies emphasizes the importance of this chant-like delivery.

75  Criterion Channel interview.

76  Ibid.

77 Akerman brings out some of these resonances in a video installation she made called "Self-Portrait/ Autobiography: A Work in Progress" (which I saw at Bozar in Brussels in 2022). The installation consists of six screens with scenes from her films, three of which display images from *D'Est* and two images from *Jeanne Dielman*. Their coordination suggests that while Jeanne might be working in isolation, her movements have roots in Eastern European practices. Perhaps this is also what is motivating her, to keep up a vanishing form of life. It would make her another of the characters who is single-handedly trying to construct an inhabitable "home."

78 Criterion Channel interview.

79 On the relationship between pleasure, sensibility, and "'luxury" in the film, see Alice Blackhurst, *Luxury, Sensation, and the Moving Image*. She argues that the film invites "a sensual, haptic and indeed luxurious' re-engagement with the body in an era of acute physical remoteness and virtual reality" (p. 16).

80 Skvirsky, *The Process Genre*, p. 206.

81 In "'Like a Musical Piece': Akerman and Musicality," Adam Roberts compares Akerman's visual compositions to musical scores. He writes, "Akerman raises all gestures to an equal standing, and organizes her material musically in order to maintain her grip and command that we might see every gesture as it is for what it is. Without such compositional methods to peel a potato might then be simply to peel a potato" (p. 137).

82 *I Don't Belong Anywhere*.

83 Ibid.

84 See Rita Felski, "The Invention of Everyday Life," for a discussion of ambivalence in feminist theories of everyday life, which oscillate between seeing the everyday lives of women as a source of value on the one hand, and seeing them as grounds for suspicion and problematization on the other (pp. 93–4).

85 Akerman also seemed to think that calling it feminist implied that her film was critical of the life that Jeanne leads, rather than trying to depict it "lovingly." But Akerman wavered on this front. As she admitted, "I don't think a man would have made this film."

86 See Ros Murray, "Revisiting Jeanne Dielman."

87 "Getting Ready for the Golden Eighties," interview with Gary Indiana.

88 Several critics have commented on this line. Emily LaBarge writes, "Akerman is not the arbiter of her characters'—or her actors'—interiority. This eternal mystery is something she leaves to your imagination" ("Chantal Akerman's Elusive Interiors"). Christine Smallwood emphasizes Akerman's own contrast between mystery and secret, saying that a mystery can be solved, whereas "a secret can, or should, never be revealed" (*La Captive*, p. 151).

# 3

# Love

## All Night Long

It is nighttime, the screen mostly dark. We watch a series of clipped scenes, fragments of stories, the gestures dimly familiar. A woman in a low-cut red dress paces the length of her apartment, picks up the phone, and dials a number. She hangs up as soon as she hears a male voice, whispering "I love him, I love him" into the empty room. Another woman descends a pair of stairs followed by a man. She asks him his name, he asks her hers, and they fall into each other's arms. They are scenes of waiting, of yearning, of peering through windows, of knocking on doors. They are also scenes of meeting, of embracing, swaying to music, strolling entwined. Some of them are tender, like that of the couple that was in the midst of watching TV, the man dozing on the couch, when the woman suddenly gets up and suggests that they go dancing in the city. Some of them hint at conflict, like that of the woman skulking out of the house when she is approached by a man from behind who grabs her elbow and hurries her down the street.

I have been describing Akerman's *Toute une nuit* (1982), a film set during a single night in Brussels and structured as brief vignettes that rarely develop and never overlap. What binds the characters together is this night, this city, and a love song that sweeps through the film as if carried by the summer breeze.[1] Even though these are isolated scenes, they mount a cumulative effect. We might not know much about these people beyond their fleeting moments together or apart, but we do get a sense of a pattern. We recognize these as the significant moments of romantic love, the images we associate with the way that falling in (or out of) love is represented.[2] In Marsha Kinder's words, "we find the traditional vocabulary and moves of the melodramatic narrative: the rendezvous, separations and reunions, the romantic triangles, balcony scenes and slow dances, the taxis, telephones, and cigarettes, the waiting women and even waiting men—in short, the problems of the couple."[3] It has sometimes been described as the universal language of love or its corporeal equivalent.[4] With only a few exceptions—two men lying in bed, a mother smoking a cigarette while her daughter calls to her off-screen—these are the images of heterosexual romance.[5]

*Toute une nuit* is a departure for Akerman, and it can seem like a long way from *Jeanne Dielman*. Since it consists mostly of climaxes, it is less interested in the "images between images" and more interested in the images themselves, the very stuff of mainstream movies. But to describe the film as action-packed would be misleading. All we get is a reel of highlights without a narrative that could lend them significance, which means that these scenes lose some of the drama they might have otherwise evoked. Ivone Margulies describes them as proliferating "micronarratives" that recall and defy cliches.[6] In a sense, *Toute une nuit* is testing how little you need in order to suggest a story, a mystery. Is a sequence of two of three shots sufficient? What does it take to see these passing shapes, many of their faces eclipsed by shadows, as distinct individuals with intriguing lives?[7] These ministories unfold in such rapid succession that they can also lull the audience into a meditative, maybe even soporific state. A student told me that while watching *Toute une nuit* at the theater, he enjoyed a restful nap. This is just to say that this film is also challenging, calling for a different level of attention from the kinds of movies from which such scenes could have been culled. But it is a turning point for Akerman. The mood has brightened, now pervaded by an optimism.[8] And her subject matter has changed. She is now making movies about romantic love.

For those who stay awake, *Toute une nuit* can also be pleasurably absorbing. It is a beautiful film, one of Akerman's most visually arresting. As Adam Roberts has described it, "*Toute une nuit* is a rich feast, not suitable for the impatient diner. It demands care and attention to fully digest."[9] But its pleasures are conjoined with a sense of unease, for Akerman dwells on these significant moments just long enough to invite us to wonder not only about these figures's lives but also about how unique any amorous encounter really is, and by implication, how unique the feelings that seem so singular to a person in their grip. Falling in love can feel unprecedented, like discovering a hidden reality beneath the surface of the everyday. Sooner or later, however, it often dawns on us—or at least those watching us—that we are living out a story we have seen, heard, or read somewhere before. Love has its conventions. In a slim volume called *Desire/Love*, Lauren Berlant asks: "What does it mean about love that its expressions tend to be so *conventional*, so bound up in institutions like marriage and family, property relations, and stock phrases and plots?"[10] They are asking what it means about love that it tends to lapse into romance, "a particular version of the story of love," and a version that reduces life's possibilities to just one plot.[11] Berlant's question highlights the close connection between conventions in two senses: conventions as institutions, and conventions as modes of expression, stock phrases and plots. Both senses suggest that romantic love is bound by a rather tight script.

According to Arlie Hochschild, this script includes the "feeling rules" that govern our emotional responses and thereby influence which possibilities we go on to pursue. In *The Managed Heart*, she argues that our intimate interactions are pervaded by feeling rules, steering us away from some feelings toward others by communicating (sometimes implicitly, sometimes explicitly) what is appropriate and what is inappropriate to feel. Feeling rules subject any unruly feelings to convention. Although feeling rules can change, they do not altogether disappear, keeping feelings subject to some rule or another. She provides the example of a bride who expected her wedding day to be the happiest of her life and then struggled in the face of the fact that she was disappointed during most of its course.[12] The bride is enacting several scripts at once. There is the narrative script that true love ought to lead to marriage and so forth. Then there is the emotional script about how she ought to feel at each stage of her conventional life story. If we are operating under an optimism norm, we will conflate what we can realistically expect to feel with what we ideally desire to feel, which means that we will be alarmed and dissatisfied whenever our feelings do not meet this high standard of fit.[13] Berlant would have called this form of optimism cruel.

Hochschild insists that adhering to feeling rules is not only a matter of performance, of giving the impression that the bride has the appropriate feelings in order to convince others that she does. It is also a question of feeling itself, of convincing herself that she is happy on her wedding day by finding techniques for managing her heart, for inducing happiness in its depths, for instance by staring into the groom's eyes until all sources of discontent fall away. For Hochschild, this is an example of the kind of invisible emotional labor that we perform on a regular basis. She writes that when it comes to the roles we assume in our personal lives, we tend to "expect to have more freedom from feeling rules and less need for emotional work; in reality, however, the subterranean work of placing an acceptable inner face on ambivalence is actually all the more crucial to them."[14] A social role—and here Hochschild lists as examples that of *bride, wife, or mother*—"is partly a way of describing what feelings people think are owed or are owing."[15] These roles are constituted by feelings, propped up by expectations about their constancy and fortitude. Is it a coincidence that they also happen to correspond to the key stages in the unfolding of the romance plot?

During the period that followed *Toute une nuit*, Akerman turned to scripts as metaphors for the romance plots and feeling rules that influence character and audience alike. While *Toute une nuit* may not present images between images, it has been described as a "film between films," also as a *liminal film*.[16] On the one hand, *Toute une nuit* retains an experimental structure: it is fragmentary and repetitive, hence "non-teleological, non-classical."[17] On the other hand, it anticipates a very different kind of experiment for Akerman, her venture into *genre*. I am thinking specifically of two genre films she went on to make: *The Golden Eighties*, a musical from 1986, and *A Couch in New York*, a romantic comedy from 1996. People who are only familiar with her work from the seventies are often surprised when they find out that Akerman directed a musical and a romantic comedy. But she was always open about her wish to reach a wider audience and disappointed that she did not make a box-office hit. At that point in time, it was probably too late for her to shed her reputation for being difficult and to attract viewers who were not already familiar with her earlier work. But the two films are still infused with Akerman's sensibility, tinged with her characteristic melancholy. Plus, they provide Akerman with a different structure within which to play and to test the boundaries of the medium.

In *Pursuits of Happiness*, Stanley Cavell considered two different ways of picturing genre in film. According to the first picture, a genre can be compared to an object with certain properties, which would mean that any genre can be defined in terms of these properties. A film would then be the member of a genre if it exhibits the properties in question. According to the second picture, which Cavell promotes, a genre is the inheritance of certain conditions, procedures, subjects, and goals. A film would then be the member of a genre if it studies this inheritance and assumes responsibility for it.[18] Cavell invokes Wittgenstein's metaphor of family resemblances in order to spell this out. As the metaphor suggests, we can identify certain films as belonging to the same genre because they resemble one another, even if we cannot draw up a list of properties that they all share. But Cavell adds an important amendment. His point is not just that the members of a genre look *like* each other. Rather, he is claiming that they look *at* each other, for "they *are what they are* in view of one another."[19] This makes genres self-reflective. Cavell even thinks that genre films strive "toward a state of absolute explicitness, of expressive saturation."[20] New members can contribute something genuinely new to the genre not by adding new properties to an evolving list but by amplifying an awareness of a genre's inheritance. For Cavell, this also means that genres can exhaust themselves, namely, when there is nothing left to lay bare.

*Toute une nuit* is a film about love in which self-reflection has reached a fever pitch. Perhaps a better way to describe it would be to say that it is not a film about love but a film about film about love. As Dominiek Hoens puts it, it is "as if the film were saying about itself, 'Look, I'm a film.'"[21] Although *Toute une nuit* is genre-defying, we might follow Cavell's suggestion and consider it as belonging to the genres from which it draws because it is studying the inherence of romantic love and cinema's role in shaping its conventions.

In one of the vignettes, a young girl who bears a striking resemblance to Akerman herself enters a café and asks a much older and taller man to dance. He initiates a dance at a distance, but the girl steps decisively toward him and throws her arms around his neck. While he is unsure of where to place his hands, she seems to be enacting a fantasy she has gotten from somewhere, probably from the movies (Figure 16).[22]

Romantic genres carry the burden of wrapping things up. Whether they end on a positive or negative note, they are telling us what a happy ending looks like and what to do or avoid in order to arrive at it. This means that they play a part in reducing life's possibilities to just one plot. As *Toute une nuit* indicates, the ideal of romance can be a source of loneliness and alienation for those who do not conform to its desires or for those who are simply unlucky in love.

FIGURE 16 Toute une nuit *directed by Chantal Akerman 1982. Collections CINEMATEK—© Fondation Chantal Akerman.*

*Toute une nuit* also explores the techniques that romantic genre films employ in order to prime or hone our emotional responses. In the enveloping darkness of the movie theater, it can become difficult to watch a comedy or drama indifferently, without being swept up in the feelings that the film is depicting. The audience is touched, amused, angered, relieved. By communicating to us when these emotional responses are appropriate, genres serve as training grounds or instruction sites for feeling rules. *Toute une nuit* is a film about the darkness of the movie theater that is so similar to the cloak of the night. Even though it does not aim to manage our hearts, it does track the ways in which this usually happens at the movies. I am thinking specifically of its use of Gino Lorenzi's *L'Amore Perdonera*, a love song that echoes throughout the film. It is a song that both expresses and triggers passion, in the viewer and in the figures on screen. We become trained to expect it. And whenever we hear the song, we can be sure that romance will soon follow.

For example, the song is heard in the distance while a man and a woman are sitting at a café. It grows louder and then fades away, as if through the open window of a passing car. Although the man and the woman's eyes do not lock, we can feel the mounting tension between them (Figure 17). They place money on their respective tables and get up to leave. The man suddenly pivots and falls into the woman's arms. A few scenes later, we watch them clutching each other, this very same song blasting, presumably from a jukebox. In the last scene of the film, we hear the song again while a different couple dances at dawn in the hallway of an apartment. It is the same woman who was wearing the low-cut red dress, calling a man and hanging up on him earlier in the film. This time the song does not come from any obvious source within the scene. She is telling her dance partner what she loves about another man who is not present. The phone rings, bringing the song to an abrupt halt. As the soundtrack confirms, they have been jolted

FIGURE 17 Toute une nuit *directed by Chantal Akerman 1982. Collections CINEMATEK—© Fondation Chantal Akerman.*

out of their trance, the tension between them vanished. Akerman is shifting back and forth from using the song diegetically to non-diegetically, suggesting a continuity in its effect on and off-screen.

Akerman is drawn to love not only because it is a conventional theme in cinema, but also because it provides her with an opportunity to revisit her central oppositions. In *Toute une nuit*, we watch several couples that have settled into a domestic co-existence, some happier than others, but the film also includes a series of women fleeing into the outer world. A woman packs her suitcase while her husband is sound asleep. She puts on lipstick, leaves the house, and roams the empty streets until she arrives at and checks into a hotel. At dawn, she sneaks back into her marital bed, pretending that she is only now waking up beside her husband. Even the countless embraces throughout the film are hardly commonplace encounters. They are a little bit too ardent, intense. Through repetition and exaggeration, Akerman suggests an overwhelming passion, an aggression lying in wait, an ineradicable vulnerability, all part of love's allegedly explosive potential.[23]

Genre films that have romance as their subject matter are a case in point. They often build tension through love's pull in opposing directions, its drive toward and away from home. Without both sides of romance, there would be no plot, no dramatic climax. To reframe Berlant's question in Akerman's terms would be to ask: what does it mean about love that it is expressed and represented as both conventional and unconventional, bound up in institutions like marriage but also opposed to them? If this opposition is already inscribed into romance, can it ever veer off-script? Although Akerman's genre films pose this question, to which I will now turn, her own attempt at an answer informs a different set of films, which are less about love and more about desire.

## The Eighties

Akerman spent the early eighties trying to find funding for a musical. When Gary Indiana asked her whether she was really going to make a musical, her answer was unequivocal: "It's going to be a big musical, all music, but not all the time singing. It's going to have five hundred actors, in a set we'll construct. It's going to be about love, and commerce, about people who are working in a shopping center. Hairdressers, vendors, shopgirls, snack bar girls, these people."[24] Her musical would look glossy and smooth, and feature song and dance. Akerman even wrote the lyrics and cast a pop star, Lio, in a main role, though it is ironically a role in which the famous singer never sings. It was going to be set inside a mall called Galerie de la Toison d'Or, or Mall of the Golden Fleece, a reference to the arcade in Brussels where her parents ran their leather goods store. At first, she was calling her musical "La Galerie," though it later turned into *Golden Eighties*, a title that kept an allusion to its specific location, as well as to its lustrous surface.[25] Once it saw the light of day, it enjoyed a release at the Champs-Elysees and in Parisian suburbs, though it wasn't as big of a hit as she had hoped.[26] Because Akerman was having trouble finding sponsors, she decided to make a different version in the interim.

*The Eighties* was to serve as a "pilot" for *Golden Eighties*, intended to promote the project. It has the appearance of a making-of documentary because it is composed of footage from rehearsals and auditions, concluding with a brief trailer for the finished product. But it is not exactly a making-of documentary in the strict sense, standing in contrast to *Autour de Jeanne Dielman*, which would be a better exemplar of this genre. Many of the actors we see in *The Eighties* don't reappear in *Golden Eighties*, at which point she was working with a different cast. So we are not in fact seeing the making of the finished product, but a provisional, eventually abandoned stage along the way. Moreover, *The Eighties* came out three years before the film it was announcing.[27] As Gwendolyn Foster puts it, "Akerman inverts the stages of the usual practice of releasing a film and then later releasing a documentary on the making of that film."[28] And because it presents this process of making a film in a jumbled form, it has also been described as an experimental film in its own right, as well as a melodrama that is only occasionally punctured by song and dance.[29]

*The Eighties* is *Golden Eighties*' unpolished, disheveled older sibling. Some viewers like this one better than the one that came next. Akerman herself said that it was "possibly more joyous than the final film."[30] She keeps its unkempt quality, even in the trailer at its end, the one that is supposed to preview how the musical would eventually look. For example, it features a scene during which a row of female hairdressers is singing a song while washing the hair of a row of male customers. The scene never made it into the final version. It is ecstatic, giving the audience a little flavor of the mood to come. But if you look closely, you might notice that one of the hairdressers is so distracted by the singing that she is practically drowning her customer in water, spraying it all over his face. This is not just an example of sloppy acting. It can be read as a comment on this highly contrived conjunction of working and singing.[31] The term "deconstruction" is often mentioned in connection with this film.[32] This is how J. Hoberman captures what it could mean in this context: "It's not just that *Les Annees 80* [*The Eighties*] breaks down a musical into its components, Akerman also uses those elements to alter one's perception of the whole."[33] Because Akerman recorded and released *The Eighties* before *Golden Eighties*, she is in effect deconstructing something that had not yet been constructed by unraveling unsewn seams.

Though we cannot assume that an audience watching *Golden Eighties* is familiar with *The Eighties*, since the latter continues to be harder to track down, their order in her filmography speaks to Akerman's approach to the musical she went on to make. In Akerman's words, "between a script and a movie, one must go through a whole landscape. *Les annees 80* [*The Eighties*] cover the time spent in this landscape."[34] One way to describe it would be to say that it is comprised of the resources out of which the film is ultimately composed—the voices, bodies, costumes, sets, postures, movements, and also emotions that serve as its raw material. Between a script and a movie, there is a reality that must first be reshaped into another. Although the finished product does not represent this reality in any direct sense, it has its origin in a world outside the film, so it cannot avoid engaging with it, however artificial it becomes. Akerman shows this process of building a filmic world by beginning with the most minimal resource: feeling and its expression.

The film opens with a black screen.[35] We hear a woman's voice repeating over and over again: "At your age, grief soon wears off." This is a line about feeling that communicates when to feel grief and for how long. It implies that if at your age grief does not soon wear off, you are not grieving correctly. Another woman's voice (presumably Akerman's, though the screen is still black at this point) is instructing her in intonation, in how to express the feeling that belongs to such an utterance. It should not be said too emphatically or subduedly. The tone has to be just right, just above a whisper. At first, we don't have any context for this line. We don't even have a face to attach to its speaker. But when we hear this line again at a later point as part of the trailer, we recognize it as a line from a script of the romance plot. We now know that it is said by an older woman who is comforting a younger woman in matters of heartbreak, telling her not to confuse the end of young love with the end of the world.[36] Because the film is so rough and ready, genuine feeling often gets in through its cracks, putting us in touch with whatever it is that the actors are bringing to the project.

Akerman's instructions introduce feeling rules while at the same time exposing them for what they are.[37] For example, Akerman tells an actor to dash a "commercial smile." Also, when we first get to see Lio up close, Akerman comments, "Your face is very vivacious . . . even so, you have more difficulty conveying emotion." Presumably she is referring to emotion conjured by means of a technique, rather than emotion flickering spontaneously across the pop star's vivacious face (Figure 18).

The film also incorporates gender norms while at the same time exposing them for what they are. The camera zooms in on a pair of feet trading combat boots for high heels. During an extended scene, we watch a series of actors walk across a hallway, practicing a feminine gait. *The Eighties* seems to identify gender with performance, maybe even suggesting that gender just is performance.[38] It contributes to unmasking gender norms by taking us quite literally behind the

FIGURE 18 The Eighties *directed by Chantal Akerman 1983. Collections CINEMATEK—© Fondation Chantal Akerman.*

scenes. Hoberman concludes that this is a film about "how women learn to play roles," including the role at their center, that of director played by Akerman herself.[39] This puts it into conversation with *Autour de Jeanne Dielman*, where we watch the very young Akerman learn on set how to give useful instructions to the more experienced Seyrig.

*The Eighties* concludes with a woman singing a song about love, repeating over and over again that love is stronger than anything, while dancing through a waltzing crowd (Figure 19). The song comes to an abrupt halt when Lio walks toward the camera, wearing a white dress, her face stained with tears. Is this young grief that will soon pass? Is love stronger than anything? Does repeating a line make it more persuasive?

There is a cut. We are now on a rooftop with a panoramic view of Brussels. Akerman reads her acknowledgments, ending with "to next year in Jerusalem," an allusion to the Passover Seder prayer. In context,

FIGURE 19 The Eighties *directed by Chantal Akerman 1983. Collections CINEMATEK—© Fondation Chantal Akerman.*

this line can be read as a reference to the finished musical that is to come next year or the year after, and maybe also to the Jewish aspect of its story, which is not yet explicit in this pilot. But the line might have an even wider scope, referring to an "impossible dreaming," the abiding fantasy of home coming.[40] Here it shows up as the fantasy of completion, of wrapping up a project, of finding enduring love. Although *The Eighties* pursues this fantasy as a perfected movie about a tale of a love that will not end in grief, it does not seem to be fully convinced that either shall come to pass.

## Golden Eighties

With *Golden Eighties*, Akerman finally realized her dream of a big musical about love and commerce. It is a sparkling object, a constructed world nearly without cracks, disconnected from the messy landscape it had to cross in order to get there. It is, moreover, a film that shows love to be subject to the very same forces that were at play in its making. I find *Golden Eighties* highly enjoyable to watch, more so with every viewing, but I also cannot deny that it is rather bleak. As Ivone Margulies puts it, "paradigmatically abstracted in *The Eighties* and frozen in a caricature of spontaneity in *Window Shopping* [*Golden Eighties*], the musical is for Akerman the cheerful form of a basic perversion."[41] It is also a little too much, a little too repetitive and excessive. *Golden Eighties* leaves ample room for wondering about the value of the very thing it is putting so cheerfully on display.

There is Sylvie, owner of the snack bar, who receives love letters from her fiancé in Canada describing its extravagant riches. Then there is Mado, who works at the hair salon and is in love with Robert, the son of Madame and Monsieur Schwartz. Pascale, Mado's friend, used to date Robert and still has feelings for him, but she is trying to put them aside in order to be there for her friend. Robert instead loves Lili, who runs the hair salon where Mado and Pascale work. Although Lili is seeing Robert on the side, she is involved with a married gangster named Monsieur Jean, who is financing her hair salon. In a fit of jealousy over Lili, Robert decides to propose to Mado, and the two of them become engaged. But Robert cheats on Mado almost immediately and eventually leaves Mado the day before their wedding when Lili returns to the mall in order to win him back. Meanwhile, Robert's mother Jeanne Schwartz runs into an American man named Eli at the clothing store where she works together with her husband and recognizes him as the same man whom she had met after she was liberated from a concentration camp. Eli now tries to talk her into leaving her life behind, and she is tempted, though she ultimately refuses.

*Golden Eighties* represents a bifurcated world. One part of it is literally below ground, the world of the mall, which consists of four businesses—the snack back, the hair salon, the clothing store, and the movie theater—where the romantic drama unfolds. It is a world bathed in a bluish light, making everyone look icy, maybe a bit ill. The people in this world often complain of being cooped up, trapped in this place, though they move incessantly within its walls, sometimes elbowing each other in massive crowds. Though we know that the inhabitants of this below-ground world only work there, for us it is as if they never get to leave. In any case, we never see them anywhere else. Because the stores have large windows, everyone can observe everyone else, making the mall ripe for gossip. Sometimes these people seek refuge in the movie theater, where they are no longer as visible to each other. But there is also another world, the one above ground, the world outside the mall. For most of the film we don't know very much about this other world. We do not get to see it until the very end. We know that it exists only because we watch people going up and down the staircase. The top of the staircase is occasionally illuminated in a warmer, brighter light, for example when Lili makes her first entrance, as if descending from a stage (Figure 20).

At one point, a crowd of men arrives with wet trench coats and dripping umbrellas, singing a song called "It's Raining." For those trapped inside the mall, the rain represents a reprieve they do not get to enjoy, a little taste of what it must be like above ground. They fantasize about real weather brought down from the sky, unlike the

FIGURE 20 Golden Eighties *directed by Chantal Akerman 1986. Collections CINEMATEK—© Fondation Chantal Akerman.*

relentless heat due to a broken air conditioner. We don't actually follow anyone to this other world, not until the last few minutes of the film, when three mall-dwellers make their way upstairs.

Akerman is working with a hierarchy of spaces with clear-cut partitions. There is a heavy iron door separating the inside and the outside of the mall. The world inside the mall seems not quite real, replete with images. Akerman is going for a high degree of artificiality through tacky costumes, catchy songs, and a chorus of "idle males" who sing a running commentary.[42] The below-ground world contains an even less real world, namely, the movies on view at the theater, which only highlights the mall's artificiality, reminding us that we are watching a movie in which people spontaneously erupt into song and dance. Akerman's camera draws this connection. Several of the characters look directly into it, as if performing for our benefit.[43] If this below-ground world is thoroughly artificial, it seems to be relying on a contrast with the real or natural world. Although we might expect that the above-ground world would then have to be the real or natural world, this expectation is in fact disappointed. The world above ground suggests a mall writ large, allowing for window shopping at even fancier brands.[44]

Akerman's exaggeration of artificiality is continuous with the genre of musicals.[45] Many musicals represent a deliberately utopian world, one that does not resemble our own, but one that we can recognize as an ideal. For example, *Oklahoma!* shows a world that is constructed to be "natural," a cooperative community and cornfields as far as the eye can see. Many musicals also include a self-conscious, even ironic relationship to their own artificiality. I am thinking of *Singing in the Rain*, which takes place mostly on a Hollywood film set. As a musical about the transition from silent to sound film, it draws attention to itself as a fruit of this transition, but also implies that sound film is to be celebrated as an instance of progress.[46]

I am also thinking of Jacques Demy's *Umbrellas of Cherbourg*, which is without a single line that isn't sung.[47] When the male lead sings to his friends that he is about to take his girlfriend to see an opera, one of them responds singingly that he prefers going to the movies because there isn't so much singing in them. Despite this joke at its own expense, *Umbrellas of Cherbourg* is also making a case in favor of its own artificiality by showing that it can become highly absorbing, even heartbreaking. The last two musicals are self-referential, admitting up front that they are showing a constructed world, one soaked in occasional rain.[48] But they are not cynical. They even conjure utopian feelings, as Richard Dyer puts it, showing "what utopia would feel like rather than how it would be organized."[49]

*Golden Eighties* is disillusioned by comparison. There is the economic recession, the utility and tax bills, the rising prices, and the dwindling customers that do little more than peer through shop windows. Commercial pressures are felt throughout the mall. As Mado is preparing for her wedding, she admits that she is fed up with the emotional labor of "smiling at those women all day." The hairdressers seem to have a hard time balancing working and singing, their dancing consisting mostly of manhandling their customers' hair. There is the pressure to please men, shown through women running out of the clothing store frustrated by the options available to them, the dresses too feminine, too revealing, or just too plain. There is also the shadow of the Holocaust. Eli reminds Jeanne that at the time they met, she had said that the camp had killed all feeling in her. When later in the film Jeanne is holding the weeping Mado in her arms, she ties together these loose ends. She says, "You'll meet a man who loves you. How could it be any other way?. . . This crisis can't last. As long as there is food to eat we'll make it through. If not, there'll be another horror. And this time no one will be spared. But that won't happen again. Never again. Things always work out."[50]

Like other musicals, *Golden Eighties* is preoccupied with the marriage question. It even opens with a reference to the wedding of a hairdresser, Sonia, who does not return until the very end of the film. But its attitude toward marriage is also disillusioned. Like *Toute une Nuit*, it shows conventional emotions to be conventional. As Steven Shapiro puts it, "In [*Golden Eighties*], each person who falls in love suffers the same embarrassment, gets swept up in the same elation, is tormented by the same jealousy, and ends up feeling the same bittersweet regret."[51]

Unlike *Toute une Nuit*, the stakes are material. Everyone inside the world of the mall seems to be acutely aware that marriage is less a matter of romance and more a matter of financial stability and that this remains the case especially for women. For example, when Sonia finally returns to the mall, she admits to the other hairdressers that marriage is "OK, but the pay is lousy."

To the extent that *Golden Eighties* is about romantic love, it fails in every single case. Jeanne does not run away with Eli, choosing security over passion. Sylvie is disappointed by the prospect that her fiancée might actually come back from Canada, presumably preferring the fantasy to its realization. When Robert dumps Mado, she breaks down in tears, but her first thoughts are about the wedding gifts and about marriage in general. Although the passion between Lili and Robert intensifies, no one seems to believe that they will live happily ever after, least of all Lili.

In a scene that says a lot about how love looks inside the mall, Lili approaches Jeanne incognito, wearing sunglasses and a scarf wrapped around her head. She admits that she has returned to the mall because she still harbors feelings for Robert. Jeanne warns Lili that Robert will make her miserable, but Lili reassures her that she is clear-sighted. Lili insists that Robert has what she wants. With the others, she felt trapped. As Lili puts it, "You know me, I need space and sunlight," adding that Robert is so young, presumably when compared to her previous two lovers, Monsieur Jean and subsequently Eli, with whom she takes up after she leaves her job at the mall. It is not that Robert is the man of her dreams. Rather, he has the advantage of being young, hence associated with space and sunlight. But youth is hardly a basis for optimism. By the time Robert delivers his own speech about the imperative of boundless expansion, we see that Robert is well on his way to becoming another version of his father, who delivered a similar speech earlier in the film. Although Jeanne warns Lili that "love only brings misery," she decides to help them reunite, explaining that Robert will "make Mado more miserable than he'll make you." In the mall world, you are well advised to pair up with whoever will make you less miserable, or whomever you will make less miserable. The world Akerman has constructed is not just self-aware; it is not even taken in by its own images. Its inhabitants already know that the love plot leads in the best-case scenario to the eternal recurrence of the same.

Does stepping into the daylight of the world above ground lead to new insight? When Mado, Jeanne, and Monsieur Schwartz finally do make it to the street, they gain new information (Figure 21). On the street, they run into Eli, who had seemed to be the most romantic of all the characters in the film, but who is now accompanied by a

FIGURE 21 Golden Eighties *directed by Chantal Akerman 1986. Collections CINEMATEK—© Fondation Chantal Akerman.*

woman he introduces to the three of them as his wife. In the below-ground world, Eli had insisted that he could never get over Jeanne. In the above-ground world, he does not give Jeanne a second glance. It is not exactly a shocking discovery, and it only serves to confirm an assumption shared by the married couple, that love is both less and more serious than young people believe.

It is less serious because it does not really matter with whom you end up (the heart is "fickle"). It is also more serious because it does matter that you end up with someone (the heart "has to love somebody"). As the three of them watch Eli and his wife walk away, Monsieur Schwartz provides a sober assessment of love's non-optional place in life. Spouses are like dresses, some look better on the rack, some are too expensive, but everyone will have to buy a dress because "you can't walk around naked." He adds that "if people did that, we'd be out of business." He is talking about his own business of selling dresses, but also about the business of making movies like the one in which his speech is featured. Through him, *Golden Eighties* seems to be admitting that it is also peddling the love plot.

## A Couch in New York

If people are surprised to find out that Akerman directed a musical, they are usually even more so to find out that she directed a romantic comedy, *A Couch in New York* (1996). As Tamar Jeffers McDonald puts it, "the romantic comedy is one of the most *generic* of genres, heavily reliant on stock elements, personae and even dialogue ('I love you!')."[52] Both musicals and romantic comedies have their conventions, but they have given rise to different traditions. Akerman was in good company when she made a musical that pushed the boundaries of the genre. She was not in any company when she attempted a similar strategy with a romantic comedy.[53] This is not to say that *A Couch in New York* does not have its predecessors. Critics have noted Ernst Lubitsch's *The Shop Around the Corner* and Nora Ephron's *Sleepless in Seattle* as films that laid the ground. *Sleepless in Seattle*, which came out three years earlier, was an especially obvious source of inspiration. Like Akerman's film, it features a couple that spends a large part of the story apart. It also reckons with the genre's inheritance by including scenes of watching movies about people falling in love.[54] In Akerman's film, the female lead goes to see a romantic movie with a friend. While her friend finds the movie terrible, she keeps repeating how much she loved it, how moved she was by it.[55]

But Akerman's romantic comedy not only nods to the tradition in which she is participating, which other romantic comedies do as well. She also accentuates the genre's strict rules by flouting them, thus straining our willingness to accept what we are watching as a romantic comedy, or at least as a successful instance of its kind. *A Couch in New York* might be entertaining, but it is emotionally unaffecting. This has led to the widespread consensus that it is a flop. In her review for *The New York Times*, Janet Maslin called it "pleasant but unaccountable fluff."[56] Other adjectives used have been flat, stiff, labored, forgettable, clumsy, and brave.

The film did have its fans at the time of its release, and in recent years, some critics have urged its reassessment.[57] To me, it seems that what you think of *A Couch in New York* says a lot about what you think of this genre. If you are evaluating the film by its rules, then it might be a flop. If you see the film as "studying" its rules, then it might be a hit. Of course, this shift in perspective assumes that it is possible to put expectations aside when watching a film that looks on the face of it to be just another romantic comedy.

Akerman described its plot as a "double fish out of water." A dour psychoanalyst, Henry Harriston (played by William Hurt), is overwhelmed by needy patients and so decides to take out an ad in a newspaper for a short-term apartment swap, looking to trade his New York loft for a place in Paris. Meanwhile, the bohemian dancer Béatrice Saulnier (played by Juliette Binoche) is overwhelmed by needy suitors when she reads Henry's ad and decides to take up his offer. The two swap apartments without meeting in person. Henry arrives to a cluttered and noisy apartment in the Parisian neighborhood of Belleville that Béatrice left in a rush, her underwear and wet footprints covering the floor. Béatrice arrives to an impeccable but sterile apartment in Manhattan, which she quickly turns into a lively mess.

Both the needy patients and the needy suitors continue to show up at their respective places, disrupting their peace of mind. While Henry is struggling to keep Béatrice's suitors at bay and to avoid turning into their psychoanalyst, Béatrice begins treating Henry's patients by impersonating Henry's replacement. She turns out to be better at it than Henry. When Henry decides that he's had enough of the chaos and returns to New York, he finds his patients, as well as his sleepy dog, "completely changed." He decides to impersonate one of his own patients under the name John Wire and to allow Béatrice to treat him. The two fall in love, though Béatrice does not realize that he is the person whose apartment she is inhabiting until the very end, when they reunite in Paris.

A question to consider is why Akerman decided to make a romantic comedy in the first place. She associates this time in her life with the death of her father, which would make this film her final effort to please her father with commercial success.[58] It suggests that she was indeed going for a blockbuster, which would mean that *A Couch in New York* failed by her own lights. Her experience of directing the film was disappointing from start to finish, and she was so dejected by the negative feedback the film received that she even entertained giving up filmmaking for good.[59] But there is something so deliberately idiosyncratic about *A Couch in New York* that I cannot really believe that Akerman was trying to make a blockbuster, though it is possible that she just grossly underestimated the constraints of the genre. In any case, *A Couch in New York* is very much another "Chantal Akerman's film." The fact that it is in many respects so continuous with Akerman's other films suggests that Akerman always remained far less limited than the genre in which she was working.[60] What makes this specific film so satisfying is its fusion of elements that no one else would have thought to combine.[61]

There is Akerman's signature style: slow pace, long takes, vapid dialogue.[62] At times, *A Couch in New York* feels like a Woody Allen comedy in slow motion, its awkward moments surrounded by periods of silence. A frequently cited example is a conversation between Béatrice and the doorman when she first arrives at the building in New York. The doorman tells her that he's always loved dancers, and Béatrice asks him why, to which the doorman has no reply. "Perhaps it's because . . . oh no, I don't know either, I don't know you well enough," Béatrice volunteers. The purpose of this scene seems to be to show us Béatrice's unstudied candor and her distaste for small talk. She wants to get to the bottom of things. This makes her refreshing, charming, and un-American. But the scene goes on for too long, forcing us to sit with the discomfort between them, finally releasing us when she turns her attention to the beauty of the elevator. She returns to his comments when she eventually concludes that it must be his "character" that explains his love of dancers, just like the dog's "character" explains his sleepiness. This scene can be contrasted with another. Béatrice calls Henry on the phone to tell him that she is returning to Paris. We only hear Henry's contribution to the conversation, and he is repeating everything she is supposedly saying without leaving her any realistic time frame in which to say it. This exchange could have been taken directly from *The Shop Around the Corner*. Not only does it allude to the fast-talking comedies of a previous era, it also serves as another element in Akerman's preference for non-naturalistic acting.[63]

There are also Akerman's recurring themes that distinguish this film from others in the genre. The first is that of displacement: two people in unfamiliar environments, trying to navigate worlds to which they do not belong. The second is that of housework. Henry and Béatrice are shown mostly in each other's apartments, often performing household chores—Henry wiping Béatrice's tabletop, Béatrice vacuuming Henry's living room floor. The third and most striking theme is that of mothers. In *A Couch in New York,* Akerman has found another outlet for her preoccupation, now justified by the practice of psychoanalysis. When Béatrice finally meets Henry in person and finds him to be inscrutable, she wonders whether he is such a "difficult case" because he does not love his mother, and she is relieved to discover that he does indeed love his mother and that he is willing to describe his mother and her hands in great detail. In a line that seems to express Akerman's own state of mind, Béatrice tells Henry, "For me the worst thing about mothers is that they grow old and die." We don't see Henry's mother, or any mother for that matter, but the film takes on board the possibility, which Akerman seems to find eminently plausible, that mothers might be the key to our dysfunctions, romantic and otherwise.

*A Couch in New York* includes explicit reflections on love and its conventional representations. One way to place the film in conversation with *Golden Eighties* would be to say that it provides a different answer to the question: why is it the case that the heart has to love somebody? *Golden Eighties* suggests an economic answer, the need to sell dresses and movies about love in order to put food on the table. *A Couch in New York* suggests a philosophical answer, the need for another need. During a brisk stroll through the park, Béatrice's friend Anne paraphrases a famous quote by Lacan, that loving is giving something you don't have to someone who does not want it. As soon as she says it, it starts pouring, and the two women are drenched in rain. The quote articulates a version of a trope to be found in commonplace conceptions of love, that to love is to seek another half, a person who will fill a hole. When I love someone, I am putting my own lack on display, or in Lacan's formulations, it is with this lack that I love. What I want is someone who isn't lacking in the same way, someone who can fill me up with a plenitude. But Lacan's quote suggests that what I find through love is another self with their own hole, someone who can offer me only their own lack. Love turns out to be an exchange of lacks, which neither wants but both are doomed to get. Because love confronts us with this lack in ourselves and in another, it also speaks against character as something stable and fixed.

At first, this structure of love is not exactly evident in *A Couch in New York*. It seems to be a working premise of the film that love presupposes difference: if love makes two into one, then that which is to be unified must initially be divided. Akerman takes this to the extreme by making the two people who fall in love not only inhabitants of different worlds but also bundles of opposing traits. Henry is serious, morose, withdrawn, and uptight; Béatrice playful, cheerful, sloppy, and carefree. In the course of the film, Henry undergoes an abrupt radical transformation. First, he shows up at his apartment to discover that elements from his life have been "completely changed." His dog is no longer lying around tired all day. He can even detect a complete change in one of his patients, presumably from the way this man carries himself as he walks down the hall. Second, Henry is himself also completely changed, starting with his wardrobe, which he has to give up once the taxi driver drives away with his luggage. He remains on the dour side, but he is no longer so stiff, even accepting and appreciating the lively mess that Béatrice has introduced into his apartment. Meanwhile, Béatrice undergoes a comparably gradual transformation. She is turning herself into a psychoanalyst, clothing herself in Henry's wardrobe, and overcoming her indifference to men, which had driven her suitors so crazy. The film suggests that if these traits can be so easily shed, they must not be anchored in anything that we might call character.

During their first encounter, Béatrice and Henry are not confronting each other by means of their opposing traits. When they finally meet in person about halfway into the film, he enters his own office to find her back turned to him. She is busy cramming from a book. He lies down on his couch; she sits down on his chair. They are not looking at each other; they are not even in the same shot. Instead, the camera moves back and forth between their faces, tracking the subtle changes in their expressions. No information is exchanged between them, only yeses and sounds of approval. This scene might be intended to show the absurdity of putting a psychoanalyst on the couch, since this psychoanalyst cannot break out of his professional role in the chair. But it might also be suggesting that what draws them to each other lies below the level of conscious awareness. Henry is not attracted to Béatrice because of her quirkiness, and Béatrice to Henry because of his pensiveness.[64] They don't even have an opportunity to register the differences in their personalities. After the session is already over, Béatrice follows him into the elevator and mentions that he is so "different" when compared to other men. What she is referring to is that he is a mystery to her, which could mean that the mystery is masking a character to be discovered or that the mystery is masking a hole, a lack. But the session itself is less ambiguous. After a lengthy silence, Henry closes his eyes and inhales. Béatrice's eyes are darting. Like a dog, she is catching a whiff.[65]

Critics of this film have often complained about the lack of chemistry between the two main characters, which is sometimes explained by the lack of chemistry between Akerman and her two main actors, Juliette Binoche and William Hurt.[66] The whole time you are watching their interactions, you have the feeling that there should be a visible spark, a connection that we can see as clearly as Henry can see his patient's complete change. This feeling that something is missing is compounded by the script and its absence of meaningful conversation. Henry and Béatrice trade inane phrases from start to finish, which they echo back and forth. But it is also possible that whatever is missing is missing for a reason, or better yet, that it is missing in order to make room for another layer of connection. In Rose Capp's words, "Whether Akerman is filming the gestures and perceptions of her characters in a strange city or whether she is tracing the movement of that strange dance called falling in love, she is alive to something that is alien and disconcerting: the sensations that take people out of themselves, shake them up, disturb or even annul them."[67] Since these sensations are internal to the space between two people, why do we expect that their chemistry will be visible? No film can convey scent, the film's central force of attraction. But the same issue might arise even if we were in the presence of the characters on screen. As one of the patients sums up, even if you smell heavenly to the one who loves you, how can you be one hundred percent sure that (to everyone else) you don't stink?

Unlike other romantic comedies, *A Couch of New York* avoids the marriage plot. The film refers to the institution of marriage only through Henry's engagement to Lizbeth Honeywell, who shows up at Henry's apartment and catches Béatrice vacuuming the living room floor. The fiancée assumes that Béatrice must be Henry's new love interest, concluding that "he has such eclectic tastes, a housewife." Though Béatrice is not a housewife, the film does suggest that romance culminates if not in marriage, then in mundane routine. Consider the final scene, during which Henry and Béatrice encounter each other on adjacent balconies in Paris. They seem to sense each other's presence, though the overgrown vegetation obscures their view. Béatrice tells the man she assumes to be Henry Harriston that she is in love with John Wire. Eventually, Henry ceases to disguise his voice and parrots Béatrice's idiosyncratic formulations, which allows her to recognize him as the man she had been describing. In the most awkward scene in the entire film, they push the many plants aside, confess their love to each other, and exchange a friendly kiss. Béatrice decides to climb onto his (or her) balcony, and Henry helps her along by dragging her across. This would have been the moment for passion, a moment worthy of *Toute une Nuit*. What we get is the immediate lapse into the everyday concerns of a long-term couple. Henry tells her that he messed things up and strewed her clothes across the floor in order to make her feel at home. He admits to some changes to her place. He tells her, "I did a lot of work, I repaired the leak." As he carries her into the bedroom, he does so as her already domestic partner. The final words seem to announce the predictable death of romance: "This is your bed. We'll have to share it now."

There are at least two features that drew Akerman to romantic love and its genres. First, romantic love is infused with feelings that are ungovernable but also disciplined by Hochschild's "rules" that make them and their outer expressions conventional and identifiable. Anyone watching a romantic movie can tell at which moment the two characters fall in love, when it is that they feel grief, jealousy, regret. Although the figures on screen are attracted by a supposed mystery in each other, to a viewer they wear their feelings on their sleeves. It seems to me that part of the pleasure of watching a conventional love story is indulging in this discrepancy between what is visible to us and what is visible to them. In any case, it is a different kind of pleasure from that which an Akerman film usually yields, since Akerman tends to opt for characters that are hard to read even to those watching from a remove.

Second, Akerman was clearly interested in romantic love because of an irresolvable tension at its heart. Romance is supposed to bring us to a home from which we will then long to escape only to seek another home that would strike us as no less confining. This suggests that there is something about the structure of romantic love that makes it comical, and that maybe comedies are especially well suited to represent this structure even if few of them take us past the altar. It would explain why the two genres that Akerman picked were on the lighthearted side.

If we take Akerman's own approach to romantic love as our starting point, we might in turn ask whether philosophy has shown an interest in love's comical side in the way Akerman has. Some philosophers have developed concepts that point in this direction: Nietzsche on eternal recurrence, Kierkegaard on repetition, and Kant on unsocial sociability. But the philosophy of love as an academic subfield has on the whole shied away from that which makes love at least a little bit ridiculous.[68] It is telling that a philosophical approach that has come closest takes its orientation from film. Cavell's *Pursuits of Happiness* doubles as a study of romantic love (and its culmination in marriage) and of romantic comedies. His focus is on comedies of remarriage, which he thinks bring the nature of marriage into view. According to Cavell,

> marriage takes a willingness for repetition, the willingness for remarriage . . . only those can genuinely marry who are already married. It is as though you know you are married when you come to see that you cannot divorce, that is, when you find that your lives simply will not disentangle. If your love is lucky, this knowledge will be greeted with laughter.[69]

The romance plot, or the marriage (or remarriage) plot, can be hilarious and it can be heartbreaking. As Akerman's ventures show, whether it is the one or the other might depend not only on your luck in love but also on your taste in and for genre.

## Notes

1. The city is not explicitly identified as Brussels, but it was filmed in three locations in Brussels. Catherine Fowler in "*All Night Long*: The Ambivalent Text of Belgianicity" discusses the significance of Brussels as the backdrop of the film (see pp. 80–1) and Akerman's allusions to Belgian art, specifically Magritte.
2. The formulation comes from Margulies, *Nothing Happens*, p. 178.
3. Marsha Kinder, "The Subversive Potential of Pseudo-Iterative," p. 12.
4. The film is often compared to Roland Barthes's *A Lover's Discourse*, "a grammar of love composed of thematic fragments which analyze seminal moments of the lover's experience (jealousy, the awakening of desire, mourning for the lost lover, etc.)" (Schmid, *Chantal Akerman*, p. 68). The obvious difference is that there is very little speech in Akerman's film.
5. The inclusion of a scene between daughter and mother, and specifically the decision to cast Nelly, suggests that such love is also a kind of romance.
6. Margulies, *Nothing Happens*, p. 178.
7. According to Kinder in "The Subversive Potential of the Pseudo-Iterative," *Toute une nuit* emphasizes the endlessly repetitive quality of these encounters. She suggests that the film even implies that similar scenes recur every night, which would rob this particular night of its singularity. Margulies has instead stressed that Akerman is not reducing these figures or events to stereotypes or generic categories but that she "recovers the uniqueness of passion by setting it up against the notions of repetition and cliché" (*Nothing Happens*, p. 178). Margulies describes this uniqueness in terms of the first-personal form that desire takes. Darlene Pursley in "Moving in Time: Chantal Akerman's *Toute une nuit*" makes a similar point: "It is within the repetitive movements of these banal romantic clichés that [Akerman] succeeds in recovering the qualitative intensities that lurk beneath them" (p. 1197).

8   In an interview for *Cahiers du Cinema* in 1982, Akerman claimed that the viewers "divide themselves into two camps: some say it is a very sad film, others find that it gives energy, that it makes you want to go out, that it produces a kind of cocaine effect. When I see it, I feel that too: it makes me want to live strongly [vivre fort]." Quoted in Dominiek Hoens, "Nothing Personal, Love: on *Toute une nuit*" https://www.e-flux.com/notes/533908/nothing-personal-love-on-toute-une-nuit.

9   Roberts, "Blogging," in the *Chantal Akerman Retrospective Handbook*, p. 193.

10  Lauren Berlant, *Love/Desire*, p. 7.

11  Ibid., p. 6.

12  Arlie Hochschild, *The Managed Heart*, pp. 59–62.

13  Ibid., note on p. 61.

14  Ibid., p. 68.

15  Ibid., p. 74.

16  Fowler, "All Night Long," p. 69.

17  Janet Bergstrom, "Disappearance in the Films of Chantal Akerman," p. 98.

18  Cavell, *Pursuits of Happiness*, p. 28.

19  Ibid., p. 29.

20  Ibid., p. 30.

21  Dominik Hoens brings out this self-reflective aspect of the film https://www.e-flux.com/notes/533908/nothing-personal-love-on-toute-une-nuit.

22  This is a point that Bergstrom makes in "Disappearance in the films of Chantal Akerman," p. 98.

23  Although I agree with Margulies that *Toute une nuit* maintains an emphasis on the singularity of passion, it is difficult to pinpoint in the film. Is it that it feels qualitatively different in each case? Is it that it arises under different circumstances for each character? Is it that it is mine and not yours?

24  https://www.artforum.com/features/getting-ready-for-the-golden-eighties-a-conversation-with-chantal-akerman-208022/.

25  In the United States, it was released under the title *Window Shopping*.

26 Schmid, *Chantal Akerman*, p. 78.

27 Gwendolyn Foster calls it a "simulacrum" ("The Mechanics of the Performing Body in *The Eighties*").

28 Ibid., p. 134.

29 Lucy Fischer claims that it is part melodrama, part musical (*Shot/Countershot*). As Jerry White writes, "The film, then, can be approached not by trying to understand what it unambiguously is but by noting all the things it isn't; it is never fully one genre or another" ("Chantal Akerman's Revisionist Aesthetic," p. 61).

30 Pajama Interview.

31 Margulies remarks on "work sliding into mess" in connection with a different scene (*Nothing Happens*, p. 191).

32 See, for example, White, "Chantal Akerman's Revisionist Aesthetics." He also emphasizes the role of play in this film and describes the images as being "gamelike" (p. 59).

33 Hoberman, *Vulgar Modernism*, p. 149.

34 Quoted in Foster, p. 146. Also in Hoberman, *Vulgar Modernism*, p. 149.

35 Many have pointed out that this is a denial of visual pleasure. Margulies has described it as an "exposé of the subtleties of performance" (p. 185).

36 Fischer (*Shot/Countershot*) claims that this new context makes the same scene into a parody: "what at first seemed melodramatic now seems comic, as the artificiality of the situation is revealed" (p. 168).

37 Foster makes a similar point: "*The Eighties* deconstructs norms of behavior that are designed to obscure the constructedness of emotion. Those norms dictate that we smile, for example, even when we might be experiencing anger, hostility, or boredom" ("The Mechanics of the Performative Body," p. 135).

38 Foster draws a comparison between this film and Judith Butler's concept of performativity (pp. 132-3).

39 Hoberman is referring to Akerman's own performance in the film in *Vulgar Modernism*, p. 149.

40 Roberts, "Blogging," in the *Chantal Akerman Retrospective Handbook*, p. 196.

41 Margulies, *Nothing Happens*, p. 191, italics mine.

42 This phrase comes from Cathy Fowler, "Harnessing Visibility."

43 Fowler describes a scene during which Lili seems to be singing to Monsieur Jean, but keeps looking at the audience until he catches on and looks into the camera in bewilderment.

44 Steven Shaviro draws a connection to Plato's cave: "The incongruity of emerging into the 'real' world like this, after an hour and a half spent in the claustrophobic perfection of the mall, is dazzling. It is sort of like an inversion of Plato's myth of the cave: we go upstairs from the unreal world of commodified forms, to arrive at the irreducible facticity of the empirical everyday" ("Cliches of Identity," p. 17). I see more continuity between the two worlds, since both are commercial.

45 It calls to mind Susan Sontag on camp, which she describes as, in essence, a "love of the unnatural: of artifice and exaggeration" (Sontag, "Notes on Camp," p. 275). Foster mentions "camp humor," p. 133.

46 *Singing in the Rain* alludes to *Jazz Singer*, which is usually described as the first sound film. It features synchronized singing and deals with Jewish assimilation into American culture.

47 For a comparison to Jacques Demy, see Fowler, "Harnessing Visibility": "One could even go so far as to suggest a homage to Demy in Golden Eighties since this film shares Demy's sense of the harsh reality bubbling below the utopian surface." See also Shaviro, "Cliches of Identity," p. 11.

48 On these references to rain, see Fowler, "Harnessing Visibility."

49 According to Dyer, this utopian sensibility stands in a contradictory relation to the world that is being depicted in the film. He describes this as a contradiction between a musical's representational and non-representational, specifically musical, elements ("Entertainment and Utopia," p. 231).

50 Kelley Conway, "Lyrical Akerman," interprets this statement as follows: "In the wake of the Holocaust, the film suggests at several points that romance is a luxury one cannot afford" (p. 153).

51 Shaviro: "Cliches of Identity": "We would like to believe that our romantic experiences are unique. But in fact, they are all pretty much alike. That's why it is so easy to tell when somebody is in love. We all recognize the conventional signs" ("Cliches of Identity," p. 14).

52  Tamar Jeffers McDonald, *Romantic Comedy: Boy Meets Girl Meets Genre*, pp. 10–11.

53  McDonald argues that there were experimental romantic comedies in the 1970s, citing Woody Allen's *Annie Hall* as an example. What makes these romantic comedies departures from the norm is that they included realistic elements that stand in the way of a happy ending. But this is clearly not Akerman's strategy. As we will see, *A Couch in New York* is even less "realistic" than standard romantic comedies, not because of its plot, but because of its form.

54  "In invoking the older romance, *Sleepless in Seattle* wryly acknowledges both its own fictional status, and its place within a tradition of films about fate and love" (McDonald, *Romantic Comedy*, p. 1).

55  Unlike in *Sleepless in Seattle*, we are not told which movie they watch.

56  https://archive.nytimes.com/www.nytimes.com/library/film/111997couch-film-review.html.

57  Dominik Païni was a fan at the time of its release, and Stephen White defends it in "Akerman's Revisionist Aesthetic" for showing "the radical potential that classical form can contain without being ruptured outright" (p. 63).

58  She mentions this convergence in the Pajama Interview.

59  Schmid, *Chantal Akerman*, p. 148.

60  "Rather than a directorial aberration, *A Couch in New York* incorporates the director's key stylistic and thematic preoccupations within the broad parameters on a mainstream romantic comedy." https://www.screeningthepast.com/issue-13-auteurism-2001/a-couch-in-new-york%C2%A0-chantal-akerman-and-sex-in-the-city.

61  See Gabriela Almeida: https://lwlies.com/articles/a-couch-in-new-york-chantal-akerman-romantic-comedy/.

62  Jerry White, Adrian Martin (https://www.adrianmartinfilmcritic.com/reviews/c/couch_new_york.html).

63  This is a technique that Akerman also uses in other films, such as *Family Business* and *Meetings with Anna*.

64  The manic pixie dream girl, a term coined by Nathan Rubin in 2007, refers to a female stock character in film whose sole purpose is to enliven boring men. Although there are elements of this character in Béatrice, the film suggests that Henry's attraction to her is not based on her quirky

personality (https://www.avclub.com/the-bataan-death-march-of-whimsy-case-file-1-elizabet-1798210595).

65 In one of the many obscure statements in this film, Béatrice claims, "I really think that the smell is very deep, very interior" when referring to the dog.

66 See, for example, Adrian Martin, https://www.adrianmartinfilmcritic.com/reviews/c/couch_new_york.html.

67 https://www.screeningthepast.com/issue-13-auteurism-2001/a-couch-in-new-york%C2%A0-chantal-akerman-and-sex-in-the-city/.

68 Philosophers have focused on questions such as: Do we have reasons for love? What do we love in another person when we love them—their general qualities, their universal humanity, or their brute singularity? Why is love so partial and selective, and should we love everyone?

69 Cavell, *Pursuits of Happiness*, pp. 126–7.

# 4

# Desire

## Movement of Desire

When Akerman was asked why she had decided to make films, she reached for the word that struck her as most appropriate: "It was a desire, a strong desire, too strong," followed by a chuckle.[1] She was expressing her frustration with the question, as with many of the other questions posed in this interview, which happened to be the same one during which she decided to break the rules and light a cigarette indoors. But Akerman does repeat the word "desire," designating it the driving force behind her work, and describing it as a desire powerful enough but also overpowering. She presumably meant that she had a strong, even too strong, desire to make films, but her clipped answer leaves its exact object unspecified. She also presents the desire as detached from any personal pronoun. She does not say, *I had a desire*, but simply, *it was a desire*, as if from elsewhere. In this way, her answer discloses something about how she sees herself. When she looks back on what kept her going in the face of obstacles that she could not have anticipated when she first got started, she suspects that an impersonal, outsized desire had singled her out.

Akerman began thinking about the nature of desire and its cinematic representation as early as her first feature-length film, *Je Tu Il Elle* (1974), a film she later described as "foolhardy."[2] It started its life as a novel a few years before and was shot within a week shortly after her return to Belgium from her first extended stay in New York. According to Akerman, the story had a personal basis: "I hitchhiked back to Brussels to see the girl, Claire, who's in the film, and I had all sorts of adventures with the truck drivers who picked me up. It was dangerous. But that's how we lived at the time."[3] In *Je Tu Il Elle*, Akerman fashions this inspiration into the story of a young woman identified as Julie in the final credits and played by Akerman herself. She had originally planned to cast someone else in this main role but realized that she preferred the uneasiness of her own body for the part.[4] In the film, her physical presence predominates. It is a body with a vast hunger, sometimes for food and sometimes for something else, setting her on a journey that takes her from a room to the road to the apartment of a former lover, a woman.

Beginning with *Je Tu Il Elle*, Akerman made a series of films that reflect her self-understanding even more intimately than those I have considered so far. This list includes *Meetings with Anna* (1978), *I'm Hungry, I'm Cold* (1984), *Portrait of a Young Girl at the End of the 60s in Brussels* (1994), and *La Captive* (2000). On the one hand, these are films that explore the nature of erotic desire, specifically queer desire. On the other hand, they also bring to light Akerman's own desire to keep making films against all odds. In fact they are interested in connections between creative pursuits and bodily appetites, or between collaborations among women and attractions between them. These films are not exactly members of a genre. In many ways they even showcase just how far Akerman was willing to stray from conventional forms of storytelling. But I am nonetheless tempted to group them together as Akerman's take on the "road movie" because they are characterized by a movement without a determinate end.

I am taking the term "road movie" loosely, since the road in question need not extend far beyond a given city or even a narrow set of streets.[5] As elsewhere, Akerman invokes and challenges the opposition between leaving home and staying put. Akerman also returns to the fraught relationship between interiority and what is visible on screen. Desire bridges the gulf, since desire is both inner and outer, something subjective as well as something manifest in our bodies. In these films, desire works as an internal drive that spurs movement from one place to another, setting a person on a certain path. Each film tracks the development of a desire that becomes increasingly difficult to pin down. When it comes to desire, who or what is its subject, and who or what its object?

Others have also noticed continuities between some of these films. Gilles Deleuze identifies *Je Tu Il Elle* as the beginning of Akerman's contribution to a "cinema of bodies," which for Deleuze is a turn to bodies—their facial expressions, their ceremonial rituals, their theatrical gests—over and above character. He traces it to films such as Godard's *Pierrot Le Fou*, where the two main characters adopt exaggerated versions of everyday gestures. According to Deleuze, Akerman's films belong to the same style because in them "a woman's body achieves a strange nomadism which makes it cross ages, situations and places."[6] Brenda Longfellow identifies *Je Tu Il Elle* as the first of Akerman's films that connects erotic desire with the figure of the mother. As Longfellow notes, "Desire in these films circulates around the maternal body, around the variable presence and absence of the mother, around the enduring gaze of the daughter at the mother."[7] As Longfellow underscores, from as early as *Je Tu Il Elle* it becomes clear that Akerman's interest in desire is often another iteration of her enduring fascination with mother-daughter relationships and their far-reaching effects into adult life.

*Je Tu Il Elle* pays homage to road movies through its division into three segments that track the steps of a journey through space.[8] In the first segment, which Akerman calls *the time of subjectivity*, Julie is alone in a room. She removes most of the furniture, takes off her clothes, and spends many days writing letters. She eats powdered sugar out of a paper bag, sometimes mechanically, sometimes haphazardly, eventually spilling it all over her sweater. In the second part, which Akerman calls *the time of the other or reportage*, Julie leaves her room, hitchhikes along a freeway, and gets picked up by a truck driver, who takes her to a restaurant, a bar, another bar, and a restroom. They eat dinner sitting side by side, Julie serving him from a shared dish and imitating his gestures.[9] Back in the truck, she gives him a hand job. Afterwards, she listens to his speech and still later she watches him shave. In the third part, which Akerman calls *the time of relation*, Julie arrives at her intended destination, the apartment of a former lover, announcing "it's me" into the intercom. The woman tells Julie she cannot stay, but Akerman wants to eat and drink. The two have sex. In the morning, Julie gets dressed and leaves without saying goodbye. It turns out that sex was just another temporary rest stop, not a step in the direction of cohabitation.

We already know that Akerman had her doubts about heterosexual romance, but do these extend to lesbian romance as well? In the context of *Je Tu Il Elle*, Akerman had ample reasons to avoid the romance plot she pursued in her later genre films. Two women who desire each other in 1974 would have faced many social and political obstacles to forming a couple. But Akerman does not turn her attention to what stands externally in their way. The one obstacle that does interest her is the dominance of the romance plot itself. I noticed that during the sex scene in *Je Tu Il Elle*, the two women are watched by two dolls, one male and the other female, pinned to the wall above the bed. Perhaps these dolls are supposed to serve as a reminder of the paradigm of romantic love outside this bedroom. This would make them part of the background that, as Sara Ahmed puts it, is to direct our desires away from queer objects onto straight lines.[10] An interviewer once remarked to Akerman that the encounter between the two women in *Je Tu Il Elle* seems violent. Akerman responded by pointing out that people expect there to be a scene justifying attraction between women, whereas in the case of a man and a woman, this question would not even arise. But in that same interview, Akerman also makes the highly general statement that "love is violent."[11] Her focus is on what unfolds in the space between two people irrespective of gender. Even in her exploration of queer desire, Akerman continues to point toward an internal dynamic that tends to unsettle, sometimes even destroy interpersonal connection.

It is tempting to read the order of the three sequences of *Je Tu Il Elle* as a progressive development from unfulfillment to fulfillment, being alone representing the most dissatisfying condition, only slightly improved by a heterosexual fling, and then fully improved by a lesbian romance. Although Akerman invites comparisons between the three segments, she is not adhering to a strict teleology. As Judith Mayne has put it, "there is no lesbian triumphalism in the film."[12] Since the film ends with Julie's departure from her lover's bed, she is as solitary at the end as she was at its beginning. It has even been suggested that the film is loopy, picking up where it left off.[13] It opens with the words "and so I left" said over an image of Julie sitting by herself in a room with her back to the camera, writing at a desk. Is the voiceover referring to Julie's departure from her lover featured at the end of the film? Or did she return to her room from another departure, maybe from another lover? When Julie is alone, she is moved to shrink her distance from her lover by traveling to her apartment. When Julie is with her lover, she is moved to seek that distance by going back to her own place. Granted, it is the other woman who asks Julie to leave by the morning. But who knows whether Julie would have wanted to stay. Maybe she wanted to leave precisely in order to be in a position to return.

It is worth noticing that children hover in the acoustic background of *Je Tu Il Elle*.[14] During the first segment, we hear their chaotic voices in the distance, and during the closing credits, a song is sung by a chorus of children.[15] As Eileen Myles asks in a poem based on *Je Tu Il Elle*, "what does/ the sound/ of children/ mean to anyone."[16] This sound could be pointing in two opposing directions. Children suggest a future that Akerman saw as foreclosed to her, a future in which she would have children of her own.[17] But children also suggest a past that Akerman was reluctant to outgrow. As she puts it, "I never grew up. I was always an overgrown child . . . I never followed my father's dream, to have a family. I stayed a girl, the daughter of my mother. . . . Sometimes I regret not having kids. Maybe I would have gone from a daughter to a woman."[18] I have to admit that I am relieved that she put this thought tentatively, though I wish she hadn't been tempted by it at all. Akerman's self-understanding as an adult child informs the character of Julie, who tends to cast the people she meets in parental roles.[19] When she parts ways with the truck driver, he bops her nose in a faintly paternal gesture.[20] When she arrives at the apartment of her lover, she expects the woman to feed her a sandwich and then another by demanding "again" (*encore*). The camera shifts to Julie's side of the room, and we watch her reach across the table and grab the woman's breast (Figure 22). It is because of angles like these that Longfellow describes erotic desire for Akerman as modeled on a daughter gazing at her mother.

Akerman famously refused to allow *Je Tu Il Elle* to be screened at a gay film festival in New York. She was often asked about this refusal and grew increasingly impatient with the question. She did not want the film to be placed inside a "ghetto," she said. She also insisted that it's a "simple love story."[21] Akerman was already inclined to reject

FIGURE 22 Je Tu Il Elle *directed by Chantal Akerman 1974. Collections CINEMATEK—© Fondation Chantal Akerman.*

labels, but maybe she also worried that this specific film's disregard for labels could get lost. *Je Tu Il Elle* follows the unfolding of a desire that is not constrained by the identity of the person at whom it is directed or by the identity of the person whose desire it is. From its shifting of perspective within the frame to its switching of objects in the story, *Je Tu Il Elle* seems to be skeptical about identity as a basis for orientation.[22] But it is also no coincidence that Akerman chose to make this point through a queer love story. I was reminded of a line from Constance Debré's novel *Playboy*, in which a woman comes out as a lesbian in middle age and leaves the life she knew behind. Debré writes about any identity, "Sometimes it works for a while. Sometimes it doesn't. Either way you have to do something with the longing, the absence."[23] *Je Tu Il Elle* suggests a similar suspicion toward identity as a stable reference point. And it does so by pursuing a desire that is wayward and unwieldy and that disrupts the continuity of its subject and its object, turning both into moving targets.

## Personal Pronouns

In her stirring study of desire, *Eros the Bittersweet*, Anne Carson investigates the idea that desire is paradoxical because to desire is to want to overcome and to want to preserve the distance that separates you from your object. She is expressing the familiar thought that erotic desire (just like its close relative, romantic love) presupposes a lack. In Carson's words, "Who ever desires what is not gone? No one. The Greeks were clear on this. They invented eros to express it."[24] This makes desire both sweet and bitter at once, sweet because it is pleasurable to reach for your object, bitter because that toward which you reach is necessarily not yet within your grasp. It means that you can taste desire's sweetness only if you are willing to endure its concurrent bitterness. To maintain the sweetness, its pleasurable state of wanting, you need to maintain the bitterness, its painful distance. For Carson, desire also bears a paradoxical relationship to time. Although it is future-directed by taking aim at its satisfaction, it would ideally want to freeze the present moment and hold onto it like a melting block of ice.

Carson's main thesis in her book is that desire cannot be kept alive solely between two people. It requires the presence of another element, a third party. The one who desires and the one who is desired cannot become members of a self-enclosed world; they must include someone else (or something else) that separates them and thereby connects them. This means that desire is realized not in the form of a couple and its two-part relation but in the form of a love triangle and its three-part relation. Searching for a third party is what Carson calls "tactics of triangulation," tactics that take place foremost in the mind of the one who desires and who wants to maintain its bittersweetness.[25] Sappho's fragment 31 provides Carson with the archetype of such an imaginative triangle. The poem is about a desire for someone observed talking to a man. The first stanza goes: "He seems to me equal to gods that man/ who opposite you/ sits and listens close/ to your sweet speaking." We can read this as a lesbian love poem, though the narrator is referred to as *I* and the beloved as *you*. It is only the intruder who is identified as *he*.

But Carson also thinks that trying to find these people's identifying features would be barking up the wrong tree. As she reads it, the poem is not about real individuals or about the jealousy the narrator feels when actually watching a man sitting next to her object of desire. Rather, for Carson, it is a poem about "the geometrical figure formed by their perception of one another, and the gaps in that perception. It is an image of the distance between them."[26] "I," "you," and "he" become placeholders for the angles of a triangle. Since the narrator is in desire's throes, the triangular shape seems to be neither accidental nor lamentable. The remainder of the poem describes the narrator's state of mind in vivid terms: fire racing under skin, blurring vision, and drumming ears, turning greener than grass. In Carson's reading of it, the poem is showing us how to keep desire internally alive (how to preserve its bittersweetness) through tactics of triangulation, namely, by making room for an obstacle to desire's satisfaction. While these tactics might latch onto something perceived, triangulation could also be wholly the work of imagination.

The third and final segment of *Je Tu Il Elle*, which Akerman calls *time of relation*, confronts the limits of desire in a physical sense. The scene showcases a relation as it unfolds exclusively between two bodies. Its famous sex scene seems to be a test case by which to explore how close two people can get. Julie and her lover are naked in an embrace, but they are not engaging in caresses or even genital stimulation. Instead, they are pressing against each other and against the bed, undulating in unison, crashing like waves. Their bodies never merge, separated by the boundary of their skin (Figure 23).

Schmid describes this scene as follows: "Akerman puts the emphasis on the concrete materiality of the female bodies which wrestle and clash in a choreography of interlocking limbs and floating hair."[27] All we hear is the rustling of sheets and gradually

FIGURE 23  Je Tu Il Elle *directed by Chantal Akerman 1974. Collections CINEMATEK—© Fondation Chantal Akerman.*

the breathing and humming of the voiceover. The scene has a duck-rabbit quality. Under one guise, it can look like a struggle, a mute wrestling match. Under a different guise, it can look like an effort to get closer than is physically possible, ideally merging into one.[28]

The scene is sexually graphic, though Akerman also remains at her signature remove. At first, we are shown no close-ups, no body parts.[29] It means that we can take in more than we otherwise would. It also means that the two women remain partly obscure to us. There is a cut. The two women become visible from a different angle, their faces close to each other, stroking and kissing. Then there is another cut, and now the lover is sitting across from Julie, spreading her legs before going down on her. The sex scene becomes increasingly legible. Although Akerman once again keeps her respectful distance, a viewer could ask themselves why they have been allowed into this bedroom. But the scene is in fact a performance that presupposes an audience because it is tailored to disrupt their expectations, both about sex scenes in film and about lesbian sex in particular.[30] It is almost as if the viewer becomes the third party in a tactic of triangulation.

*Je Tu Il Elle* devotes considerable attention to another candidate for the third party, namely, the man who picks Julie up from the side of the road. Akerman calls the segment *the time of the other and reportage*. From the moment that Julie gets into his truck, he takes up most of the screen, his face shown in dimly lit close-ups. At times we do not even see Julie in the same frame. Even when we do, she has been relegated to its edge. Her body recedes from our view. Instead, its perspective merges with that of the camera, which takes on the quality of *reportage*. She stares at his neck until he rubs it, maybe because he feels her eyes on him. In one of the few explicit admissions of desire in the film, we hear Julie's voiceover say, "I thought I wanted to kiss him." It suggests that this male character is entering the story both as a conduit that will take Julie to her lover, and also as a possible object of desire in his own right. There are indeed moments of tenderness between them. In a parking lot, he places his arm around Julie. At one point, they sit across from each other at a table in front of a tank full of fish, exchanging furtive glances that make them look like awkward lovers.

But the time spent in the company of this other does not turn out to be a time of or for relation. There is a persistent asymmetry, with one of them taking up space at the other's expense. Within the geometry of Sappho's poem, it would be Julie who sits and listens close to *his* "sweet speaking." This is especially pronounced in their sex scene, during which the man takes Julie's hand and places it over his pants with the words, "you see, this is what matters." Like Julie, we watch him and listen to him direct and narrate the hand job. After he ejaculates, he drops his head onto the steering wheel and lifts it to smile into the camera, presumably into Julie's eyes.[31] His monologue is consumed by what he thinks truly matters. He tells Julie about his wife, who first attracted him but no longer does, about his flings on the road, about his prepubescent daughter who turns him on. Since he is the other, Julie is curious. He might not provide much satisfaction, but he is her gateway into a world of men, like those sitting in a row on the stools of a bar they enter. Julie already glimpsed this male world in the first segment, when she caught a passerby peeking at her naked body. After she became the target of this look, she examined her own reflection at great length before exiting the room, leaving the glass door ajar.[32]

Although desire is visibly at work in the third and second segments, it seems to me at its most pronounced in the first. As I see it, the first segment (which Akerman called *time of subjectivity*) explores what it is like to be in the throes of desire.[33] It is sometimes interpreted as being about a young woman's mental breakdown, eating disorder, or identity crisis, but these interpretations needlessly reduce what could be meant by subjectivity in this context.[34] It is a time of subjectivity because it is a time to indulge being a subject of desire, a subject reaching for an object that isn't there, a "present absence" in Carson's sense. It is a time spent alone in a room. The segment opens with Julie surrounded by densely arranged furniture, which she claims to paint blue and then green, neither of which we see or could see, since the film is black and white. Words and images continually misalign, suggesting a mind only barely tracking what the body is doing or what is happening, jumping ahead, lagging behind.³⁵ Julie pushes the furniture out of the room, keeping only the mattress, which she moves from one spot to another. She props it against the glass door, then places it onto the floor. Her behavior might look strange, but she is just like anyone in desire's hold. She wants to be able to devote herself undistractedly to what is present only in her thoughts. It is when alone in an empty room that one can truly relish and suffer desire's bittersweetness.

It is a bitter fact about desire that it is only sweet when it involves actually reaching out toward another and not just thinking about it. Lying on the mattress, Julie starts writing letters to someone she never identifies. We might assume that these letters are addressed to the *Tu* (you) of the title, but Julie never reads them out loud. We might also assume that Julie must be writing letters to the lover she eventually visits, the object of her desire. In a moment of irony, Julie says (according to the translated subtitles), "I was very clear in what I said. First it took three pages to express myself. Then I wrote the same thing in six pages." The letters are growing in length but not in content, clarity apparently calling for verbosity, not concision. But the original French actually includes a reference to an indirect object: "I wrote them [*lui*] three pages, then I wrote them [*lui*] six pages to say the same thing." Does this disclose the gender of the absent person to whom Julie wants to devote her undivided attention? Or are we filling in many of these blanks with our own assumptions?³⁶ Although some have translated it as "he," the French itself is ambiguous.³⁷ The reference to an indirect object opens another possibility, that the title of the film refers to someone else altogether, not the person to whom

Julie is writing the letters or the person she eventually visits. At one point, the voiceover narrates, "I waited some more for it to pass or for something to happen—for me to believe in God or for you to send gloves for the cold." This *you* could be anyone. Only Julie/Akerman knows whom she has in mind.

## Meetings with Anna

In 1979, Akerman met her hero Jean-Luc Godard when he interviewed her for a magazine. Although the conversation started amicably enough, Akerman grew increasingly impatient with her interlocutor. Godard was pitting *Je Tu Il Elle* against the feature film she had recently released, *Meetings with Anna* (1978). He was claiming that *Je Tu Il Elle* was a "free film" in contrast to *Meetings with Anna*, which he kept describing as a "Gaumont film" because it had been distributed by the French studio by that name.[38] Akerman was annoyed. She pointed out that the film did not resemble other "Gaumont films," to which Godard answered even more annoyingly, "what is resemblance anyway?" When he backtracked and insisted that calling something a "Gaumont film" is not to disparage it, she called him out. How could this not be meant disparagingly if he was opposing it to making a free film? Out of his depths, Godard replied that freedom is impossible anyway, since there is no place on earth where a person can be free, and that freedom is not necessarily a good thing, the difference between freedom and its opposite apparently no different from that between left and right. The lesson here is that it's probably best to avoid meeting your heroes.[39]

The fact that Godard agreed to meet her at all indicates that *Meetings with Anna*, Akerman's last film of the seventies, was a watershed moment in her career.[40] It also happens to be my favorite, which is why I chose a still from it for the cover of this book. Akerman did not conceal the fact that the film draws from her life at that point in time. At its center is the character of Anna Silver (Anna is Akerman's middle name), a film director played by Aurore Clément, who has five brief encounters, some planned, others unplanned, while traveling to promote her recently released film.[41] Her encounters extend beyond the frame, for Anna seems to have many flings during her travels. The film is structured as a journey by train, filmed as a series of highly stylized, symmetrically composed, mostly static shots in liminal spaces. Together with Anna, we watch the landscape through the window rush by. According to Gary Indiana's description of it, the film produces "the same vaguely erotic tedium as actual train travel."[42] There is restless movement, but no progressive development. The film ends with Anna as rootless as she was at the beginning.

Anna's journey begins in Essen, Germany, where she meets a man named Heinrich and takes him back to her hotel room. Although she tells him to get dressed and leave, she agrees to visit him and meet his daughter at his home in Bottrop the following day. Next, she takes a train to Cologne, where she meets Ida, an old family friend, on the station platform. Ida questions Anna's life choices, especially Anna's twice-broken engagement to Ida's son, trying to convince her to reconsider. Anna boards a train headed toward Brussels and meets a stranger in the corridor who tells her about his high hopes for life in France, where people supposedly carry freedom in their hearts. At the train station in Brussels, her mother is waiting for her. Instead of going home, they spend the night at a hotel, sleeping side by side. The last meeting is with Daniel, who picks her up from the train station in Paris. She gives him a hand job in the car. Although they both have their own places, they also decide to check into a hotel, where Anna sings him an Edith Piaf song.[43] Daniel starts feeling unwell, and Anna runs out to get medicine. When she finally arrives at her own apartment, a slew of voicemail messages is waiting for her on her answering machine.

*Meetings with Anna* is haunted by the relatively recent past, which is referenced obliquely through ellipses and images. In one of its most striking tracking shots—which even Godard couldn't help but admire—Anna is slowly opening a transparent curtain in her hotel room, feeling its fabric with her hands, as the adjacent station comes into clearer view. She opens the window to the shrill sound of trains. The image is highly concrete yet reverberates with historical associations, which Akerman deliberately invites. The film is also haunted by a different, less specific set of associations. Many of the characters inform Anna either directly or indirectly how a woman ought to live. Ida thinks that it isn't appropriate for a woman to be so rootless, urging Anna to settle down. Daniel fantasizes that if he were a woman, he would leave the grind behind by getting pregnant and forgetting everything else. The song that Anna chooses to sing for him opens with what could be a description of Jeanne Dielman: "I wash the dishes, fix coffee with cream, I'm so busy I don't have time to dream." Anna has clearly decided against satisfying these expectations, but she is also not completely indifferent to them. When Ida asks her whether she wants to have children, Anna says that she does, maybe later. She also implies in her conversation with Heinrich that she has had two abortions, explaining that the timing wasn't right. We find out that she already knows a lot about children, correcting Daniel by telling him that one has to feed a newborn only every three hours, instead of every two.

Like Julie, Anna traverses a world inhabited mostly by men. At the hotel, Anna is immediately confronted by masculine relics: a tie left behind in the closet, lace-up shoes lining the hallways at night. Anna's heels echo as she walks past them, setting her apart.[44] She pauses in front of a pair, bending down to examine the soles before picking a couple of peas off a plate (Figure 24). We don't see any other women until the following morning, when Anna walks down the hallway and finds it teeming with maids making beds, vacuuming the carpet, and bringing fresh towels. Her two erotic meetings in the film are also with men. When Anna asks Heinrich to get dressed and leave, she remarks that they are not in love, indicating her continued attachment to the ideal of romance. With Daniel, there is at least an acknowledgment

FIGURE 24 Meetings with Anna *directed by Chantal Akerman 1978.*
Collections CINEMATEK—© Fondation Chantal Akerman.

that their inability to end up together fuels their desire for each other. Before she takes off her robe and lays on top of him, he says to her, "In a moment we'll make love, and then you'll be off again tomorrow. And I'll be left wanting you more than ever." Daniel regrets the brevity of their encounter, but his speech compares favorably to Heinrich's, in which the latter describes the deterioration of his marriage. He and his wife spent weeks sleeping side by side without feeling any desire for each other.

Anna has a distinct bearing that draws people to her, making them insatiable for more. She exhibits a total, nearly indiscriminate attention, whether directed at the leftover peas on a plate or at the intimate confessions of her interlocutors. You can see this quality of attention in the level of detail with which she describes the tie and its location in her hotel room.[45] You can see it especially in her mode of listening. When she visits Heinrich at his home, the two linger in the garden, but to call their exchange a conversation would be an exaggeration. Heinrich talks uninterruptedly for seven minutes straight, telling her how his wife left him for a dark-skinned Turk and how his best friend was forced out of his teaching post for political reasons.[46] He even provides a brief recap of twentieth-century German history, mentioning the war but not the Holocaust, and ending with the question: "What have they done to my country?" Anna does not interject. She listens intently, watching him closely with her icy blue eyes.[47] Having such a rapt audience is obviously flattering, feeding one's own sense of significance. Maybe Heinrich does not even notice that Anna has shared virtually nothing in return. At the end of his speech, he hugs her in gratitude.

Anna is an elusive presence on screen, resisting our desire to understand her. Although she is in almost every frame, Janet Maslin has described her as "so fearless and joyless she's almost a ghost."[48] After she tells Heinrich to get dressed and leave, Anna returns to her empty hotel room and stands stark naked in front of the window, looking down at the same train station at night as she did when she first arrived. The camera shows her from behind, her face visible on the pane of glass. Because Anna is physically uninhibited in a way that rivals Julie, we could get the impression that she is also baring her inner life. But Anna's nudity does not make her less obscure than a character like Jeanne Dielman.[49] She too appears to be harboring a secret that she has chosen to keep to herself—at least for most of the film. We find hints of this secret in her interminable wandering and in her repeated efforts to make a phone call to Prado, Italy. As Freud famously put it, "He that has eyes to see and ears to hear may convince himself that no mortal can keep a secret. If his lips are silent, he chatters with his finger-tips; betrayal oozes out of him at every pore."[50] For an audience, it is a question of attention. Are we watching Anna as closely as she seems to be watching others? Or are we getting distracted by the silences that puncture her conversations?

Throughout *Meetings with Anna* we find more and more suggestions that Anna's thoughts wander to one specific meeting when she is alone at the end of the day. It is an erotic encounter with an unnamed and unseen Italian woman that took place before the start of the film. Although Anna is officially traveling for work, her movements are in large part organized around this woman's present absence, circling around it even if not aiming to overcome the distance in geographical terms. When Anna first appears on screen in a crowd of passengers headed for the exit, she steps away toward a bright yellow phone booth, signaling the urgency of her desire to reach the person on the other end of the line. When she arrives at the hotel reception desk, she asks whether there is a telephone in her room. As soon as she enters her room, she initiates a call to Italy, which she is told will take two hours and which she never gets to make because she has to leave for her screening. At the next train station, she again heads for a phone booth, again without success. She never manages to get in touch with the object of her desire. In the final scene of the film, she comes home to find her voice on the machine, a moment of remote and delayed reciprocation. Anna is lying on her bed when she hears in an Italian accent, "Anna, dove sta? Anna, where are you?" Although she is back at her apartment, it is just a brief reprieve. As another voice informs her, she is about to leave for yet another series of European cities: Lausanne, Geneva, Zurich.

Anna reveals her secret only to her mother while the two women are side by side in the dark. During the one monologue that Anna delivers, she recounts that a woman came back to her hotel after a screening, and the two of them went out for a drink and a long conversation. Anna claims that she talked extensively about herself, which already sets this meeting apart. Because all the bars were about to close, the two women returned to Anna's room and started kissing. Anna says she felt nauseous, confused, and overwhelmed, but then she let herself go and found it easy. She admits to her mother, "And for some strange reason, I thought of you. I even told her so." Through a tactic of triangulation, the mother figure makes her way into Anna's imagination. Maybe she serves as a source of intensity in the face of which Anna turns greener than grass. Why did Anna think about her mother at that moment? Was she remembering her mother's body, which she embraces at the end of this scene? Was she anticipating her mother's disapproval?[51] When Anna asks her mother "Have you ever loved a woman?" she answers, "I don't know, I never thought about it." It was not a possibility she ever even considered.

It seems to be Anna's first sexual experience with a woman that brought about an internal change that comes to resemble, maybe even underwrite, her wandering through Europe.[52] According to Akerman, "It is her work that makes her travel, but one could almost say of Anna that she had a vocation for exile."[53] I am again reminded of Constance Debré's words, this time from her second novel, *Love Me Tender*: "For me, homosexuality isn't about who I'm fucking, it's about who I become."[54] Anna's experience similarly exceeds her previous possibilities, propelling her onto a road without a clear-cut beginning or ending. But Akerman wanted to distinguish this version of a road movie by emphasizing that "Anna's trip through Northern Europe is not a romantic initiation voyage."[55] It would be wrong to call hers a road of self-discovery, as if she were excavating an identity that had been lying in wait all along.[56] It seems to be instead a road of self-transformation. Akerman even describes Anna as a "heroine of the future," heralding a completely new way of being.[57] She calls Anna "a sort of mutant," "on a line of flight, which is not a flight from the world, but rather a manner of anticipating what will become our future."[58] What she heralds can be described as a radically different way of relating to that elusive object of desire, not by grabbing for it, but by roaming around it, always maintaining a respectful distance.

Akerman would probably deny that Anna is a joyless ghost. This is how she describes Anna's one-sided conversation with Heinrich: "Anna receives Heinrich's words in their difference, in their strangeness. She would appear much more human if she showed some sign of effacing or reducing difference. She could have said, for instance, I understand you . . . But she would thus have tried to take power over the Other: I understand, thus I take you—an attempt to abolish difference."[59] Anna's attentive demeanor suggests a way of life that is not driven by desire, or that has changed the structure of desire beyond recognition. It is not unlike Simone Weil's conception of attention as generosity. Anna meets Heinrich in a city called Essen, the German word for eating. If Anna were hungry, she would be moved to assimilate or absorb what she encounters. Instead, she approaches the people she meets like the leftover peas: she takes a little nibble, returning them where she found them.[60] But it would be wrong to conclude that Anna is wholly passive. She is doing something, namely, *preserving difference*. What she has surpassed is the urge to assert herself or impose herself, either by volunteering stories of her own or by assuming that she can relate to whatever others tell her.[61] Anna responds merely with a yes, or an echo.[62] Akerman suggests that it is because Anna no longer wants any of the options on the menu that she is able to stay attentive to the present moment.

## All the Boys and Girls

Akerman made two shorter films about wandering women that have the shape of love triangles.[63] Both films were made as part of anthology series for French television programs. *I'm Hungry, I'm Cold* (1984) is twelve minutes long and follows two runaways from Brussels to Paris who spend the night at the apartment of a man they met at a restaurant. *Portrait of a Young Girl at the End of the 60s in Brussels* (1994) is an hour long and follows a teenager who skips school and spends her day around town with an army deserter while secretly pining for her best friend. The two films have a lot in common. Although they feature love triangles between three individuals, specifically between two girls and a male character, they also seem to be love triangles between two girls and the heterosexual romance plot, into which they are becoming initiated. It is easy to dismiss this romance plot as stifling and inhibiting, standing in the way of realizing (or even articulating) queer desire. But what Akerman explores in these two films is how the romance plot can be enlisted to serve other ends, turning it into a foil for telling a different kind of story.

*I'm Hungry, I'm Cold* opens with a shot of Paris at night. Two unnamed girls get out of a car and are handed a pair of keys to an empty apartment, the first of many blessings the city will bestow upon them. They are eighteen years old, and as they repeated over and over again, they are hungry and they are cold. The next morning, while "aging" themselves with eyeliner, one says to the other, "I want to fall in love," and the other responds, "Me too." But their most urgent appetite is for food. They go to a café where they order two rounds of tartines and coffee, which they devour. One is already checking out one of the customers, but the other is too hungry to notice men. When they leave the café without paying, she immediately wants to eat another large sandwich. Later in the evening, they return to the subject of falling in love. They both claim that they have been a little bit in love, but that they probably have to wait for the real thing. They are approached by two guys from behind, and they turn around and slap one of them, quickly crossing the street. The two friends demonstrate their previous kisses on each other, with one admitting to the other that this kiss "would make my heart pound!" It is an erotic moment made possible by their shared fantasies.

In the most affecting scene in the film, they sing Verdi for their supper at a nearby restaurant. As Kelley Conway describes it, "They sing 'la la la' instead of lyrics, veer off-tune, and trail off into awkward pauses. And yet their performance is successful. Their audacity is riveting, and when they are asked to leave by the management, a patron invites them to dine."[64] Sitting down across from this patron, they are absorbed by the menu rather than the man and his friend, but they eventually go back to his place. Although he offers to give them his bed and sleep on the couch, during the night he gets into bed with one of them, telling her that he wants to kiss her and that he wants to love her, to which she replies without looking at him, *then kiss me, then love me*. The camera shifts to the other girl, who is in the meantime making scrambled eggs in the kitchen. She is clearly too impatient to let them cook through. As she sits on a chair, runny eggs dripping out of her mouth, she seems to be watching the sex scene taking place off-screen. We hear a piercing cry. The man asks whether it was her first time, to which the girl answers, "Yes. So that's over with." She turns to the friend and says, "Come on, we're leaving," and the two walk away, side by side.

As far as the heterosexual romance plot is concerned, we don't necessarily expect either of the girls to end up with the man they meet at the restaurant. But there are other gendered expectations at work. When they accompany him to his apartment, and especially when he slips back into his own bed, we might have expected him to be unmasked as a predator who is taking advantage of their hunger. It is Akerman's creative subversion to show that this sexual experience, even if it was probably dissatisfying, has satisfied a different purpose. The girl seems to have said yes to him not primarily because she felt under pressure to do so, but because she was eager to get it over with, to check sex with a man off her list of things to do. Now that she has accomplished this task, she can return to the pleasures of female friendship.[65] As Erin Nunoda described this film and its successor, *Portrait of a Young Girl*, these two films "exist in a space between friendship and surreptitious longings that . . . contests both straight and lesbian endings."[66] In the case of *I'm Hungry, I'm Cold*, it ends on an uplifting, but likely fleeting note. Who knows where the two friends will go, what awaits them at the end of the alleyway, or at the end of their trip to Paris.

Akerman made *Portrait of a Young Girl* for a French TV series called "All the Boys and Girls of Their Age," which commissioned directors of different generations to make films about their youth with music from the era.[67] Akerman captures the spirit of the late sixties as it appeared to a teenager like herself on its cultural outskirts, someone who lived in Brussels and not in Paris, where the upheavals of 1968 were about to unfold. The film contains specific references to a moment in history. The characters quote Kierkegaard and Sartre and discuss the changes that seem inevitable. As the main character puts it, after the revolution there won't be any more "groping," "getting married," or "dressing up." The film focuses on what it is like to be a young girl, not just at the end of the sixties, but "in a man's world" as the song that Akerman chose for it goes. On the one hand, this world contains many constraints that stand in the way of a young girl's desires. On the other hand, these constraints can also become opportunities for creative intervention.[68] It would not be a stretch to read it as Akerman's version of Joyce's *Portrait of the Artist as a Young Man*.

Michèle is a high school student played by Circe, who bears an undeniable resemblance to the young Akerman. When her father drops her off in the morning, she decides to skip school, imaginatively killing off her entire family while trying to come up with an excuse for her absence.[69] In the end, she opts for tearing up her folder and throwing it into the trash. She returns to the school gate a couple of times during the day in order to talk to her best friend, Danielle, and make plans for the evening. In the movie theater by herself, she meets a guy named Paul, a deserter from the French army. They make out, eat spaghetti, and spend the afternoon in each other's company. Later in the day, Michèle and Paul break into Michèle's cousin's apartment, where they listen to the Leonard Cohen album they stole. They seem to have sex, implied by a cut. If this is indeed what happened, it would have been Michèle's first time. Michèle then meets up with Danielle and they take a tram to a classmate's party. At the end of the film, Michèle encourages Danielle to get together with Paul, because she claims to be tired of listening to her search for a boyfriend. As Danielle walks off-screen, presumably to meet Paul who is inexplicably waiting beyond the frame, Michèle turns around and walks back by herself through an empty field.

*Portrait of a Young Girl* includes a triangle comprised of Michèle, Danielle, and Paul. Even before Paul enters the picture, however, a space has been cleared for him by the romance plot to which both girls subscribe. The first time we see Michèle and Danielle together, they go to a café where they make out with two boys. For a few seconds, Michèle stops kissing and turns around to watch Danielle, staring at her long enough for Danielle to look back. They smile at each other. As Judith Mayne describes their interaction, "the look could well be one of longing directed at Danielle, or it could be a look seeking encouragement and approval . . . when Danielle and Michèle leave the café, they talk about how disappointing the kissing was, and their conversation occupies more screen time than the actual kissing did."[70] When Michèle asks Danielle why she went on kissing the boy for so long even though she did not enjoy it, the friend replies, "I didn't want to hurt his feelings. The more I felt that wasn't it, the more I felt obligated to kiss him." The girls are in the process of internalizing what is expected of them, learning to kiss all the more passionately the less they're into it just to make sure that male feelings aren't wounded. But there is something in it for them. Kissing boys gives them something to talk about with each other. The pleasures of female friendship are the pleasures of conversation.[71]

When Paul does enter the picture, he assumes a dual role, becoming an object of desire and an obstacle to desire's satisfaction. According to Mayne's interpretation, "the film could be described as a somewhat conventional girl-meets-boy tale. But what shapes the girl-meets-boy story is the simultaneous desire, for the girl, to connect to another girl and to tell stories."[72] Among all of Akerman's men, it would be hard to find one as likable as Paul. Michèle does seem to be drawn to him and to enjoy his company. When she kisses him, we don't get the sense that she is simulating passion to avoid wounding his feelings. This suggests that her desire is not fixed and focused, but fluid and diffuse.[73] At the same time, Michèle is trying to set him up with her friend, telling him that he would probably prefer Danielle because she is more popular and has long hair. She adds, "And when she likes someone, she lights up. It's amazing." It is the first inkling we get of Michèle's hidden feelings for her friend. Maybe she is trying to cope with her pessimism that these will ever be reciprocated. But her effort to place Paul between herself and Danielle suggests that she is in a sense triangulating, putting him in the way of desire's satisfaction.

Michèle is already aware that desire is at its most intense when it is mediated by something other than its direct object. A case in point is the long conversation she has with Paul about the benefits of jealousy and about their own experiences with its agony, which Michèle claims to know intimately. As Michèle admits, "Even when I'm happy, I'm in pain . . . the more I hurt, the more I smile." They agree that one reason to kiss someone is to make another person suffer, though Michèle has qualms about this strategy. She imagines how she is going to tell her object of desire about the kiss, first with a dreamy look, then by claiming that she can't remember what she saw at the movies, finally admitting that it is because she was too busy making out. When she meets up with Danielle by the school gate in the following scene, the conversation does not go exactly as she had imagined. Michèle nails the dreamy look and tells her friend that she cannot remember the movie she saw. But at that point, they run out of words. They are simply looking at each other in tense silence until Michèle confesses that she doesn't want Danielle to go home, and Danielle responds that she doesn't either.

In the course of the day, Michèle's longing for Danielle becomes plain, but its specific target is left open-ended. Michèle herself probably does not know what she wants from her object of desire except more intimacy and more connection.[74] In the most heartbreaking scene in any Akerman film, Michèle and Danielle are dancing in the middle of a circle of classmates. After Danielle rejoins the circle and it is Michèle's turn to pick another dance partner, she looks around uneasily until her eyes resettle on Danielle. Michèle seems embarrassed to have chosen to dance with her friend twice, but Danielle flashes her a reassuring smile.[75] Eventually the song comes to an end and the circle dissolves. The camera focuses on Michèle's face as she watches her friend slow dance with a boy, James Brown's "It's a Man's Man's World" blasting. The scene is unbearably, exquisitely painful. In that moment, we are invited to share Michèle's feeling of infinite distance from the couples that surround her. But it could be a turning point, even the pivotal moment at which she comes to embrace her position as spectator. Like the director of this film, Michèle's discovers a pleasure in watching that almost compensates for the pain of being on the outside looking in.

## La Captive

At the turn of this century, Akerman directed *La Captive* (2000), her first of two literary adaptations she was able to carry out.[76] *La Captive* is officially adapted from "The Prisoner," the fifth volume of Marcel Proust's *In Search of Lost Time*, though the film was never intended to be a faithful rendition. What drew Akerman to this novel was its heightened interiority, the fact that it takes place mostly in the narrator's mind. It is about the obsessive form that desire can assume, and about the ways in which a person feeds their obsessions in order to remain in desire's grip. But Akerman was also drawn to the novel's interior setting. Because the narrator suffers from allergies, most of it takes place indoors. As she recalls, "I remembered that there was the apartment, and the corridor, and the two characters—and I said, that's a story for me."[77] The two characters, Marcel, the narrator, and Albertine, the object of his obsession, became Simon and Ariane. Akerman decided to write the script entirely from memory, leaving out the rich social world in which the events unfold. Only later did she reread the novel in order to fill in crucial details, for instance, the opaque partition separating the two parts of the bathroom in order to allow the two characters a modicum of privacy.[78]

*La Captive* also pays homage to Hitchcock's *Vertigo*, to which it alludes in its opening sequence: Simon (like Scottie) trails behind Ariane (like Madeleine), following closely on her heels, while Ariane clatters across the Place Vendome, seemingly unaware or at least pretending to be unaware that she is being followed.[79] At first, we don't know whether these two people even know each other, but a couple of scenes later we catch sight of Simon shoving Ariane into a room of his apartment, trying to hide her from a visitor. By then we realize that Ariane in fact lives with him and his grandmother.[80] Simon does not seem to have much to do. He is ostensibly writing a book about Racine, but mostly he is just stalking Ariane. Ariane by contrast has a busy life. She is an aspiring singer who spends her days in the park, at the museum, or the concert hall, accompanied by her friend Andrée and sometimes a big group of beautiful women. Simon is consumed with jealous suspicions. When these become unbearable, he decides to dump her and drives her to her aunt's house outside of the city. As Eric de Kuyper (Akerman's co-author on the script) put it, the film has "more or less a kind of 'road movie' atmosphere."[81] Not only had Simon's efforts to trail Ariane set his jealousies into motion, but the two eventually hit the literal road, swerving down the coast's winding highway. Like in Akerman's other "road movies," they are "going somewhere, going nowhere . . . " both at the same time.[82] Once they half-heartedly reconcile and check into a seaside hotel, Ariane says she is going for a swim and never reemerges from the sea.

The film opens with two shots of waves. While the credits roll, the waves come in and out of focus. It is nighttime, the image is dark. Then it cuts to waves during daytime, a group of women running into the water. The quality of the image has changed, and the sound of waves is replaced by the buzz of a projector. We are now watching a Super 8mm home movie. The camera is unsteady, moving from woman to woman, but it seems to be seeking Ariane, the least conventionally beautiful among them. Ariane steps out of the water holding her friend Andrée's waist. We shift to Simon, who is standing next to the projector, uttering the words, "I . . . like . . . you . . . a lot" (*Je vous aime bien*), which he repeats when we go back to the footage of the two women, who alternate between looking at the camera and looking at each other. The third time he repeats the same sentence, he steps in front of the projector, and his silhouette covers part of Ariane's image (Figure 25).

This last shot indicates that we will be dealing with another love triangle, this time exclusively from the point of view of its male member. Simon's obsessive desire is at the center of this film. It is his sullen face that tends to consume the screen. But in a strange inversion, Simon lives in a world that seems to be inhabited mostly by women.

FIGURE 25  La Captive *directed by Chantal Akerman 2000. Collections CINEMATEK—© Fondation Chantal Akerman.*

With the exception of his driver and a couple of workmen renovating his apartment, everywhere Simon looks he sees only women: on his screen, in his apartment, below his window.

In Kaja Silverman's close reading of this opening sequence, she argues that the referent of "I like you a lot" changes in the course of the three utterances.[83] The first time we hear it, we see Simon say the words, so we have reason to assume that Simon is referring to himself in the first person. The second time, another possibility arises, that "the first- and second-person pronouns are reversible designators for Ariane and Andrée."[84] Although the image is too grainy to tell, he could be trying to read their lips in the recording and to mimic what they are saying to each other.[85] Silverman claims that the third time, he has reentered the screen as a silhouette, thereby referring back to himself in the first person. But he also refers to both of them in the plural (*vous*), affirming "their right to address these words to each other."[86] Silverman's interpretation accounts for a surprising feature of Simon's relationship with Ariane. Even though Simon is consumed with jealousy of every other woman she meets, he seems to trust Andrée and even encourage their close friendship. This is, in fact, another element of the story that Akerman took directly from the novel, in which Marcel initially exempts her close friend from his jealous suspicions. In another scene that calls Hitchcock to mind, Simon follows Ariane through the Rodin Museum, remaining only a few steps behind. At first, Simon is visibly agitated by Ariane's aimless meandering. Once Andrée appears at Ariane's side, Simon smiles in relief and retreats. Maybe he should have been more worried about their friendship; after all, it is Andrée's name that Ariane mutters during sex with him.

There seems to be an agreement between Simon and Ariane that Ariane sleeps in her own bed but is available to him if he calls her on the phone, at which point she appears in his bedroom wearing a translucent robe. She sleeps or pretends to sleep while Simon dry humps her from behind. These are by far the strangest sex scenes in any Akerman film, but Ariane's participation in the process suggests that she has consented. She even seems to be enjoying it.[87] Maybe she likes that sex with Simon is non-invasive or non-procreative. Simon for his part only seems to be sexually interested in Ariane asleep. At one point, he asks his driver to take him to Bois de Boulogne where he picks up a prostitute who resembles Ariane and asks her to sleep (or feign sleep) in his car. But she isn't sleeping correctly, not like Ariane. Why is it that Simon wants Ariane asleep? Maybe then he can convince himself that he possesses her completely, that there is no part of her that is not at his disposal.[88] Or, maybe then he possesses her least of all because she has escaped into her dreams.

When she wakes up, she looks surprised to see him. He worries that she sees him as a stranger, but he also seems to prefer it that way. Unlike Simon, Ariane understands that desire is only sustainable if you allow the other person to become a stranger every once in a while. She tells Simon, "I love you because there's a part of you I don't know. I imagine you've this world I cannot enter." Simon answers, "I'm the total opposite. For me, love is the very opposite." Clearly, Simon does not know himself or his own views about love very well.

Simon is obsessed with finding out what Ariane truly wants, where she travels in her thoughts (and dreams). It is almost as if Simon wants to inhabit her point of view, to see the world as Ariane sees it. Of course, it is only because she is capable of concealing her desires that she continues to entice him. It is her secret inner life that makes her that obscure object of desire. It is also what makes her a desirable object of knowledge. Because Simon identifies seeing with knowing, he wants to see what is in principle not visible: Ariane's mind not as it is expressed, but as it is withheld. He seems to think that if he could just watch her when she does not know that she is being watched, he will get the full picture. He also seems to think that if he could just photograph her, she won't slip beyond his frame.[89] Kate Rennebohm describes Simon's relationship with Ariane as a form of hyperbolic skepticism.[90] Simon is trying to turn Ariane into an object that can be known by turning her life into something frozen, fixed, ideally dead.[91] Rennebohm's reading suggests that it is Simon who eventually drives Ariane to her own death not because he wants to kill her, but because he wants to pin her down.[92] It would make her death his wish fulfillment.[93]

Simon is convinced that it is Ariane's attraction to women that makes her radically unknowable to him—another element that Akerman took directly from the novel.[94] He seems to be less worried by the prospect that Ariane is having lesbian affairs than by the prospect that she harbors lesbian fantasies. Her behavior is observable, whereas her desires are not. According to Louise Hornby, it is unsurprising that Simon should focus on Ariane's attraction to women, since her alleged lesbianism is a symbol of "resistance" to and "refusal" of the world that Simon represents.[95] The film does not settle the question of Ariane's true sexuality, since it is interested primarily in the role it plays in Simon's imagination. But the film does provide some reasons for thinking that his fears are not unfounded. Ariane is visibly happier when she is with other women. Simon even overhears a conversation between Ariane and Andrée during which they discuss the sensuality of a woman's voice. Andrée then convinces Ariane to join her for a performance with the famous singer Léa.[96] Simon rushes to the opera, bolting out of the car and running up the stairs. We catch him dragging Ariane by the elbow, away from her friends (Figure 26).

Just before he shoves her into the car, Léa (played by Aurore Clément) appears on the front steps, calling out to Ariane, "See you tonight!" Ariane isn't able to reply. She does not fault Simon for this, but she also does not indulge him. When he later gropes her while she is napping and asks her what she was thinking about, she says: about nothing (*a rien*).[97] During a key scene later in the film, Ariane's face lights up when she joins a duet from Mozart's *Cosi Fan Tutte* with a woman on an adjacent balcony.[98] The other woman seems to be a professional singer, while Ariane's voice is comparably

FIGURE 26 La Captive *directed by Chantal Akerman 2000. Collections CINEMATEK—© Fondation Chantal Akerman.*

untrained. Simon catches their duet in the courtyard. His face registers the evidence.[99]

After he hears Ariane and her neighbor singing together, Simon rushes to the theater to interrogate a couple, Sarah and Isabelle. He tells them, "I am burning to know what goes on between women that doesn't between a man and a woman. I imagine . . . but I don't know . . . above all in terms of feelings, but not just, gestures too." They don't know how to explain it or what kind of explanation would satisfy him. He clarifies that what he wants to know is whether it is possible to forget that you are having sex with a man. They tell him that it is. In fact, Sarah confesses that she often forgets the person she is having sex with. "Eyes closed, you think of who you like. You are free to think of what you like." Although neither Simon nor Isabelle seems pleased to hear this, maybe they secretly prefer it this way since fantasies indicate the presence of another mind, and not just another body. Simon also wants to know whether it is "a question of bodies," namely, whether there is something about women's bodies that makes an experience with them different in kind. Since he shares a preference for women, shouldn't he be able to understand what it is like to be a lesbian? What this couple tries to communicate to him is that there is more to it than that; it is a matter of connection between two people. And as Simon's insatiable hunt for the elusive Ariane shows, he cannot even begin to understand what it would be to connect.

*La Captive* represents Akerman's most complex and overt exploration of the structure of desire. What *La Captive* highlights is an important disanalogy between erotic desires and bodily appetites. Erotic desire is not just a desire for an object to be consumed but a desire for another subject with desires of their own, desires that they can conceal. This isomorphism between subject and object destabilizes the distinction between points of view in the film. Although this is Simon's story, many have noted that it is unclear who is captor and who is captive, since Simon is also captivated by his object, captive to his desire for it. This shows desire in *La Captive* to be different from desire in *Je Tu Il Elle*. *Je Tu Il Elle* ran up against our inability to overcome a bodily boundary, the boundary of skin. In *La Captive*, at issue is our inability to enter fully into another's interiority. In fact, the film suggests that what makes someone desirable is their power to harbor secrets, to refrain from divulging them. Ariane is perhaps the most mysterious among Akerman's women, repelling any effort to look behind her placid mien. Just like Ariane's secrets enthrall Simon, they might also enthrall some of us.

*La Captive* confronts Carson's paradox of desire by taking it to a pathological extreme. Carson, in fact, wrote a short book on Proust called *The Albertine Workout*, in which she describes Proust's novel as illustrating his "theory of desire, which equates possession of another person with erasure of the otherness of her mind, while at the same time positing otherness as what makes another person desirable."[100] But the novel displays the narrator's self-conscious attempts to revive a dwindling desire by creating situations of jealousy that could spur it back to life. Marcel entertains thoughts like the following: "There must be something inaccessible in what we love, something to pursue; we only love what we do not possess."[101] In the film, Simon does not seem to know this. He is led by his desires without even realizing to what extent he is steering them. His mind spills out onto the road, merging with the paths that lead somewhere, nowhere. The film shows what happens when desire is allowed to unfurl unchecked: it implodes, dragging both subject and object out to sea. I want to be clear that Akerman herself does not endorse this theory of desire. Desire for her is not compelled to destroy its object by seizing it, freezing it, or turning it into a figment. She did say that she often felt that she lived inside a prison, which made her identify with both Marcel *and* Albertine, Simon *and* Ariane.[102] She admitted she was glad she became a filmmaker instead of a writer, her other option. Otherwise, she too might have rarely gone outside.

I want to conclude this chapter (and this book) by outlining the contours of one final thought I find in *La Captive*, as well as in Akerman's oeuvre as a whole. *La Captive* uses the trope of captivity in order to get at its seeming opposite, *freedom*, while challenging the assumption that the two are starkly opposed. As she did with so many of the obstacles she encountered, Akerman turned Proust's text into a constraint that doubles as an opportunity to do her own thing, and hence as an occasion to reflect on the freedom that she lived through her work. And like the films I have just described, *La Captive* suggests that it might be possible to desire differently, to be a subject of desire without being at its mercy, and to allow your object of desire its independence. In *La Captive*, it is Ariane who hints at this alternative.[103] At first, Ariane seems unfree, a woman trapped in a web. But by the end, we are invited to see Ariane as freer than her captor. No matter how closely Simon watches her, she can always slip down corridors into spaces where no one can follow. But like Akerman herself, Ariane does not have to stay stuck inside her own room, inside her own mind. Thankfully, there are friends for singing songs, making films, or talking philosophy.

# Notes

1 *Chantal Akerman, From Here.*

2 Pajama Interview.

3 Ibid.

4 "It was a matter of putting across a malaise . . . I started to direct an actress and soon I noticed that her perfection went against the project. I also thought [it] more appropriate . . . to oppose the mis-en-scène's rigidity with my own uneasiness" (quoted in Margulies, *Nothing Happens*, p. 112).

5 *Jeanne Dielman* can also be described as a road movie in this sense. Jenny Chamarette points out that even Jeanne Dielman "wanders from time to time" ("Ageless: Akerman's Avatars," p. 58).

6 Gilles Deleuze, *Cinema 2*, p. 196. He also mentions Virginia Woolf as a literary counterpart to Akerman. Deleuze contrasts Akerman's films that are austere and stylized (like *Meetings with Anna*) with those that involve an element of the burlesque (like *I'm Hungry, I'm Cold*).

7 Longfellow, "Love Letters to the Mother," p. 74.

8 "The different styles of the three parts—the first is indebted to 1970s performance art, the second to the reportage genre and the third offers an alternative to erotic or pornographic cinema—highlight the various stages of this journey" (Schmid, *Chantal Akerman*, p. 27).

9 Judith Mayne ("Girl Talk") writes that Julie is no longer hungry in the second segment and that her hunger only reappears in the third. She claims that Julie is serving the trucker from her own plate. But it's the third plate placed on the table, which suggests that maybe it was meant to be shared. I take Julie's gesture of serving the trucker to be an allusion not to her lack of hunger, but to gender norms.

10 Sara Ahmed, *Queer Phenomenology*.

11 *Chantal Akerman Œuvre écrite et parlée 1968–1991*.

12 Mayne, *Woman at the Keyhole*.

13 This interpretation is usually ascribed to Jean Narboni.

14 Akerman often uses the voices of children in her films. See, for example, *Letters Home*, which includes acoustic allusions to Sylvia Plath's two children. In a very early film, *L'Enfant aimé ou je joue à être une femme mariée*, Akerman cast a child actor and then regretted it.

15 Conway ("Lyrical Akerman") compares the merging of the two voices to the bodies during the sex scene, which I will discuss below. "But just as the film refrains from implying that Akerman's character will form a long-lasting couple with her ex-lover, the soundtrack suggests the maintenance of autonomy. Akerman's charming but untrained singing voice remains distinguishable from her partner's more confident performance" (pp. 143–4).

16 Eileen Myles, "inside 'i, you, he, she,'" *Chantal Akerman, Travelling*, p. 51.

17 In *No Future: Queer Theory and the Death Drive*, Lee Edelman argues that because queer sex is not reproductive, queer people pose a challenge to "reproductive futurism," that is, the imperative to contribute to the social reproduction of the status quo. As he puts it, "there are no *queers* in that future as there can be no future for queers, chosen as they are to bear the bad tidings that there can be no future at all" (p. 3). Akerman's approach to the question of reproduction is less bleak than Edelman's. See, for example, Alison Rowley, "Between Les Rendez-Vous d'Anna and Demain on Déménage," and Ros Murray, "The Radical Politics of Possibility."

18 Pajama Interview.

19 Chamarette ("Ageless: Akerman's Avatars") claims that the characters based on Akerman like Julie in *Je Tu Il Elle* resist aging by wandering.

20 Several commentators have described the gesture as "paternal," including Marion Schmid, *Chantal Akerman*, p. 30.

21 https://www.youtube.com/watch?v=zT3BDXIwuvs.

22 Margulies's reference to an "identity crisis" comes closer to what I have in mind: "Akerman's process of de-individualization results from an untenable accumulation of functions in a single body... This accumulation creates a fissure in the body's supposed unity, forcing one to read several conflicting registers of identity with equal acuity: that of author, performer, and character (*Nothing Happens*, p. 110).

23 Constance Debré, *Playboy*, p. 168. Gracie Hadland draws a connection to *Je Tu Il Elle* in her review of Debré's other novel, *Love Me Tender*: https://lareviewofbooks.org/article/absolute-sovereignty-on-constance-debres-love-me-tender/.

24 Anne Carson, *Eros the Bittersweet*, p. 11.

25 Ibid., p. 30.

26 Ibid., p. 16.

27 Schmid, *Chantal Akerman*, p. 31.

28 In Becca Rothfeld's words, "The object of any erotic fervor is always outrageously other, an anomaly on the outside clamoring to squirm in" (*All Things Are Too Small*, p. 59).

29 In her interview with Gary Indiana, Akerman makes the following remark about this scene: "It's not voyeuristic because the camera doesn't move. If the camera had moved, and picked up something, singled out something, it would have been different. But the way the camera stayed, fixed—it's very dignified."

30 Maureen Turim writes, "I see this sex scene as breaking with a still prevalent stereotype of lesbian sexuality at the time of the film's production, the 'best friends and dearest lovers' model of an ideal feminist lesbianism" ("Personal Pronouncements," p. 19).

31 Mayne (in *Woman at the Keyhole*) claims that it is this moment of the film that shows the convergence of Akerman as subject (director) and Akerman

as object (actor), since both occupy "the same metaphoric position, behind the camera."

32  Schmid writes, "Julie, at this stage in her journey, still depends on the exterior, here male, gaze to constitute herself as a subject" (*Chantal Akerman*, p. 28).

33  Mayne writes, "The scene suggests both calm and torment, peaceful solitude and turbulence" (*Woman at the Keyhole*).

34  According to Margulies, "Chantal's self-inflicted seclusion can be seen as shaping a movement of subtraction. Minimalism here becomes a willed form of defining the self" (*Nothing Happens*, p. 113).

35  Turim (pp. 11–12) and Margulies (pp. 114–18) provide interpretations of this mismatch.

36  As Mayne writes, "Much of her writing consists of a letter addressed to a person, a lover one assumes, whose gender is unspecified; but given so-called normal viewing expectations, one assumes the indirect object of unspecified gender, 'lui,' to be a man" (*Woman at the Keyhole*).

37  In Margulies, it is translated as "he" (*Nothing Happens*, p. 117).

38  About *Je Tu Il Elle*, he said "good or bad—that's not the question," maybe giving away his own assessment.

39  In later interviews, Akerman also accused Godard of antisemitism. There is some evidence of it in this interview, especially during their discussion of Akerman's unrealized project of adapting Isaac Bashevis Singer.

40  The reviews at the time were also mixed. Because this film was so polished, critics wondered whether she was turning her back on the avant-garde.

41  As Akerman describes it, she met Aurore Clément through Delphine Seyrig. Although Akerman found Clément too beautiful (and too blonde) for the part, which was based on Akerman herself, she decided to cast her in this role, perhaps for the same reason that she cast Seyrig in *Jeanne Dielman*: in order to subvert expectations.

42  "Getting Ready for the Golden Eighties," interview with Gary Indiana.

43  During the premiere of the film at Cannes, the audience started booing and throwing tomatoes when Clément began singing this song. Akerman and Clément had to flee the theater. They met Seyrig at a café. Seyrig said to Clément, "Don't worry, the film is beautiful" (https://www.criterionchannel.com/videos/aurore-clement-interview).

For a discussion of the significance of this song, see Conway, "Lyrical Akerman," pp. 144–7.

44  For a discussion of the long process by which Chantal Akerman picked Aurore Clément's shoes, see https://www.criterionchannel.com/videos/aurore-clement-interview.

45  This is something that Margulies emphasizes in her reading of the tie scene (*Nothing Happens*, p. 161).

46  Heinrich seems to make a reference to Germany's even more recent past, the German Autumn of 1977, and the height of the RAF's terrorist activities.

47  According to Margulies, "the status of her attention is ambivalent: as she listens to other characters talk, her stance wavers between concern and distant politeness in such a way that it is hard to tell the difference" (*Nothing Happens*, p. 155).

48  Janet Maslin's review for *The New York Times*: https://www.nytimes.com/1979/04/27/archives/film-les-rendezvousenigmatic-character.html.

49  As Christine Smallwood writes, "Akerman gives the viewer Anna's body but preserves her secret; she reveals everything and gives nothing away" (*La Captive*, p. 38).

50  Freud, *Dora*, p. 69.

51  When Anna mentions that she is trying to call a female friend, her mother immediately brings up Pierre, a boyfriend with whom Anna had recently broken up. Additionally, her mother tells her that they shouldn't tell Anna's father.

52  I am grateful to Amanda Lopatin for this suggestion. According to Lopatin's interpretation of this film, there is a parallel between Jeanne Dielman and Anna Silver: just as Jeanne's domestic routine is upended by an orgasm, so Anna's pattern of heterosexual flings is disrupted by this lesbian encounter, which she can't incorporate into the life she had constructed up to that point.

53  Quoted in Margulies, *Nothing Happens*, p. 162.

54  The passage draws a comparison with conversion experiences: "It's the tipping point, the Kairos, it's like the conversion of Saint Augustine, just as radical. It's not just a matter of him believing in God or me liking women, it's the fact that there's a life before and a life after" (Debré, *Love Me Tender*, p. 29).

55 Quoted in Margulies, *Nothing Happens*, p. 162.

56 Margulies claims that "Akerman makes clear that Anna's affair is a sign of freedom, rather than an exclusive sexual preference that would explain her wish to remain single" ("Echo and Voice in Meetings with Anna," p. 71).

57 Cited in the review by Janet Maslin.

58 Quoted in Margulies, "Echo and Voice in Meetings with Anna," p. 70.

59 Quoted in Schmid, *Chantal Akerman*, p. 56.

60 Margulies makes the point that Anna loses her appetite when she has to eat German food. In Cologne, she suggests to Ida that they go eat, but then decides against it as soon as she steps into the restaurant ("Echo and Voice in Meetings with Anna," p. 62).

61 Smallwood writes, "So often we rush to speak and fail to listen, or collapse the very distance that we need to see. Akerman measures that distance. There is a strong ethical imperative in her form to let other people exist— on their own terms, in their own time" (*La Captive*, p. 38).

62 While listening to a stranger on the train, Anna also responds with "so they say."

63 She also made a film about a love triangle between a woman and two men, *Night and Day* (1991).

64 Conway, "Lyrical Akerman," p. 154.

65 As Conway puts it, "*J'ai faim, j'ai froid* ultimately suggests the pleasures of female friendship. Their singing voices—similar, yet different—symbolize both their solidarity and their individuality" (Ibid.,).

66 From The Akerman Year podcast.

67 In her essay "Lesbian Minor Cinema," Patricia White suggests that Akerman is bringing together two senses of "minor," the television commission and underage characters.

68 I am especially inspired by Mayne ("Girl Talk"), who writes, "Several of Akerman's films have suggested how lesbianism upsets any fixed notions of subject/object relationships, while simultaneously suggesting that lesbianism is both inside and outside dominant practices of sexuality. *Portrait of a Young Girl* continues in these directions as well, but does something more at the same time; it evokes with great beauty and sadness the complex ways in which a girl's love for another girl inspires narrative and visual form" (p. 154).

69 According to Mayne, "The fantasy of her own death is also a fantasy of rebirth, of shedding the various institutional identities she possesses, those associated with the family and school" ("Girl Talk," p. 151).

70 Mayne, "Girl Talk," p. 151.

71 Many critics have pointed out the importance of conversation in this film. See, for example, Schmid, *Chantal Akerman*, p. 140.

72 Mayne, "Girl Talk," p. 150.

73 Schmid writes, "it may be more accurate to describe the film as a meditation on the fluidity of sexual desire and, like the earlier *Je Tu Il Elle*, as a study of an adolescent's experiment with different—heterosexual and homosexual—sexual identities" (*Chantal Akerman*, p. 141).

74 White ("Minor Lesbian Cinema") has pointed out that *Portrait of a Young Girl* is not a simple "coming out story." It refuses "predictive [narrative] in favor of an unrealized potential" (p. 411). This makes it similar in structure to *Meetings with Anna*.

75 This scene has led Turim to draw the following comparison: "A scene in bed with Paul, and the later repeated choosing of her girlfriend as partner at a joyous and sensual center of a circle dance echo the truck driver and former lover sequence of [*Je Tu Il Elle*], by giving us a similar, if more exuberant encounter with a male superseded by a non-verbalized choosing of a female partner" ("Personal Pronouncements," pp. 22–3).

76 Her other major adaptation (and last fiction film) was Joseph Conrad's *Almayer's Folly* (2011).

77 *Chantal Akerman, From Here*, quoted in Smallwood, *La Captive*, p. 16.

78 Akerman toyed with the idea of adapting this novel as early as the seventies, but she describes herself as too dogmatic at the time. She claims that when she made *La Captive*, the "only question I asked myself is the following: what remains in memory? To adapt a monument like Proust simply amounts to filming affection, emotion, and sadness" (quoted and translated in Schmid, *Chantal Akerman*, p. 151).

79 Recall that *Jeanne Dielman* dethroned *Vertigo* in the *Sight and Sound* poll.

80 It is striking that the film does not feature any mothers, only Simon's grandmother.

81 https://sabzian.be/text/la-captive-by-chantal-akerman.

82 Ibid.

83 Kaja Silverman, *The Miracle of Analogy*, pp. 150–8. Silverman draws a comparison with *Je Tu Il Elle* and its use of pronouns whose referent seems to change. According to Silverman, the "I" (je) changes from Julie to the truck driver, who starts to use it to refer to himself.

84 Silverman, *The Miracle of Analogy*, p. 155.

85 According to Louise Hornby, Simon is "ventriloquizing Ariane's own words to her companion Andrée as they share the screen" (*Still Modernism: Photography, Literature, and Film*, p. 60).

86 Silverman, *The Miracle of Analogy*, p. 156.

87 Emma Wilson writes, "The ritual, like an s/m contract, allows Ariane to find pleasure in submission" ("Unknown Deaths in La Captive," p. 92).

88 In the novel, he compares Albertine asleep to a plant, which suggests that Marcel assumes that when she is sleeping, Albertine does not lead an inner life.

89 Silverman emphasizes the role of photography in the opening sequence. Hornsby writes, "This riddle unfolds an epistemology of photographic excess and noncontinuity, which garners knowledge both by proliferating serial images and by attempting to draw ever closer to its subject, in magnified pieces" (*Still Modernism*, p. 59).

90 Kate Rennebohm, "Chantal Akerman and Stanley Cavell."

91 Rennebohm includes a critical engagement with Cavell's reference to *La Captive*, which he identifies with "the camera's invasive power of surveillance or vampirism" (*Cities of Words*, p. 118). As Rennebohm puts it, "Simon wants to make her into that which can be subject to perfect knowing and viewing—say, as in a film" ("Chantal Akerman and Stanley Cavell," p. 254).

92 There is a lot of divergence in interpretations of the penultimate scene. Schmid says that Ariane is "in all likelihood driven to suicide by her lover's obsessive need for control and knowledge" (*Chantal Akerman*, p. 152). Smallwood claims, "I think that Ariane isn't trying to die at all; she just wants to get away from Simon. She thought she wanted the life she knew, but she changed her mind; she is sick of it now" (*La Captive*, p. 175). Wilson thinks we cannot rule out that Simon actually held her underwater ("Unknown Deaths in La Captive," p. 96).

93  Rennebohm concludes that it "is a feat of Akerman's artistry that throughout the film, and despite her acquiescence, Ariane never feels caught by either the spectator or Simon" ("Chantal Akerman and Stanley Cavell," p. 262).

94  As Carson puts it elsewhere, "in point of fact, how can he possess her mind if she is a lesbian?" (*Albertine Workout*, p. 9). She is talking about Proust's narrator, not Akerman's character.

95  Hornby, *Still Modernism*, p. 61.

96  In the novel, Léa is well known as a lesbian, but this background information is left out of the film.

97  Critics have pointed out that "a rien" echoes Ariane. See, for example, Wilson, "Unknown Deaths in La Captive," p. 94.

98  Schmid thinks that we can assume that this woman is the singer Léa (*Chantal Akerman*, p. 158). But she is not Aurore Clément.

99  Conway: "The call-and-response structure gives way to the melding of the two women's voices and offers the film's most persuasive evidence of Ariane's preference for women" ("Lyrical Akerman," p. 156).

100  Carson, *Albertine Workout*, p. 9.

101  Proust, *The Prisoner*, p. 366.

102  https://www.youtube.com/watch?v=Gtob9ZMqGG4&t=289s.

103  I was inspired by Smallwood's observation that "Ariane, not Simon, is Akerman's model of the artist" (*La Captive*, p. 161).

# BIBLIOGRAPHY

Ahmed, Sara (2006), *Queer Phenomenology: Orientations, Objects, Others*, Durham: Duke University Press.
Akerman, Chantal (2002), *A Family in Brussels*, New York: Dia Art Foundation.
Akerman, Chantal (2004), *Autoportrait en Cineaste*, Paris: Centre Pompidou.
Akerman, Chantal (2019), *My Mother Laughs*, Northampton, MA: The Song Cave.
Akerman, Chantal (2024), *Œuvre écrite et parlée 1968-1991*, edited by Cyril Béghin, Fondation Chantal Akerman.
Altman, Rick (1987), *The American Film Musical*, Bloomington: Indiana University Press.
Anzaldúa, Gloria (1987), *Borderlands/ La Frontera: The New Mestiza*, San Francisco: Aunt Lute Books.
Barker, Jennifer M. (2003), "The Feminine Side of New York: Travelogue, Autobiography and Architecture in *News from Home*" (pp. 41-58) in *Identity and Memory: The Films of Chantal Akerman*, edited by Gwendolyn Audrey Foster, Carbondale: Southern Illinois University Press.
Beauvoir (1985), *A Very Easy Death*, Pantheon.
Beauvoir (2011), *The Second Sex*, Vintage.
Bergstrom, Janet (2019), "Disappearance in the Films of Chantal Akerman" (pp. 96-103), *Moving Image Review & Art Journal* 8: 1-2.
Bergstrom, Janet (2003), "Invented Memories" (pp. 94-116) in *Identity and Memory: The Films of Chantal Akerman*, edited by Gwendolyn Audrey Foster, Carbondale: Southern Illinois University Press.
Berlant, Lauren (2012), *Desire/Love*, Brooklyn: Dead Letter.
Blackhurst, Alice (2021), *Luxury, Sensation and the Moving Image*, Cambridge: Legenda.
*Bordering on Fiction: Chantal Akerman's D'Est* (1995), Minneapolis: Walker Art Center.
Butler, Kristine (2003), "Bordering on Fiction: Chantal Akerman's *From the East*" (pp. 162-78) in *Identity and Memory: The Films of Chantal Akerman*, edited by Gwendolyn Audrey Foster, Carbondale: Southern Illinois University Press.
Carson, Anne (1986), *Eros the Bittersweet*, Princeton: Princeton University Press.
Carson, Anne (2014), *The Albertine Workout*, New York: New Directions.

Cavell, Stanley (1981), *Pursuits of Happiness: The Hollywood Comedy of Remarriage*, Cambridge, MA: Harvard University Press.

Cavell, Stanley (2004), *Cities of Words: Pedagogical Letters on a Register of the Moral Life*, Cambridge, MA: Harvard University Press.

Cavell, Stanely (2005), "The World as Things: Collecting Thoughts on Collecting" (241–79), in *Cavell on Film*, edited by William Rothman, Albany: SUNY Press.

Cavell, Stanley (2022), *Here and There: Sites of Philosophy*, Cambridge, MA: Harvard University Press.

Chamarette, Jenny (2019), "Ageless: Akerman's Avatars" (54–65), in *Chantal Akerman: Afterlives*, edited by Marion Schmid and Emma Wilson, Legenda.

*Chantal Akerman: Passages*, Eye Filmmuseum, Naioio Publishers.

*Chantal Akerman, Traveling*, edited by Celine Brouwez, Marta Ponsa, Laurence Rassel, and Alberta Sessa, Bozar-Centre for Fine Arts, 2024.

Conway, Kelley (2019), "Lyrical Akerman" (pp. 139–60), *Camera Obscura: On Chantal Akerman*, edited by Patricia White, Duhram, NC: Duke University Press.

Corpas, Irene Valle (2021), "Between Home and Flight: Interior Space, Time and Desire in the Films of Chantal Akerman," *Journal of Aesthetics and Culture* 13: 1.

David, Angela (1981), *Women, Race & Class*, London: Penguin Random House.

Debré, Constance (2022), *Love Me Tender*, Semiotext(e).

Debré, Constance (2024), *Playboy*, Semiotext(e).

Deleuze, Gilles (1989), *Cinema 2: The Time-Image*, Minneapolis: University of Minnesota Press.

Despentes, Virginie (2024), *Dear Dickhead*, London: Maclehose.

Dreyfus, Hubert (2007), "The Return of the Myth of the Mental," *Inquiry* 50: 4, 352–65.

Dyer, Richard (2002), *Only Entertainment*, Routledge.

Edelman, Lee (2004), *No Future: Queer Theory and the Death Drive*, Durham: Duke University Press.

Elpidorou, Andreas and Lauren Freeman (2015), "Affectivity in Heidegger I: Moods and Emotions in Being and Time" (pp. 661–71), *Philosophy Compass* 10: 10.

Federici, Silvia (2012), *Revolution Point Zero: Housework, Reproduction, and Feminist Struggle*, Oakland: PM Press.

Felski, Rita (2000), *Doing Time: Feminist Theory and Postmodern Culture*, New York: New York University Press.

Fischer, Lucy (2014), *Shot/Countershot: Film Tradition and Women's Cinema*, Princeton: Princeton University Press.

Flitterman-Lewis, Sandy (1996), *To Desire Differently: Feminism and the French Cinema*, New York: Columbia University Press.

Flitterman-Lewis, Sandy (2019), "Ephemeral, Elusive, Impossible: Chantal Akerman and the concept of 'home'" (pp. 106–16), *Moving Image Review and Art Journal* 8: 1–2.

Forrester, Katrina (2022), "Feminist Demands and the Problem of Housework" (pp. 1278–1292)), *American Political Science Review* 116: 4.

Foster, Gwendolyn Audrey (2003), "The Mechanics of the Performative Body in *The Eighties*" (pp. 132–49) in *Identity and Memory: The Films of Chantal Akerman*, edited by Gwendolyn Audrey Foster, Carbondale: Southern Illinois University Press.

Fowler, Catherine (2003), "*All Night Long*: The Ambivalent Text of 'Belgianicity'" (pp. 77–93) in *Identity and Memory: The Films of Chantal Akerman*, edited by Gwendolyn Audrey Foster, Carbondale: Southern Illinois University Press.

Fox, Albertine (2019), "Vocal Landscapes: Framing Mutable Stories in De l'autre côté (2002) and Une voix dans le désert (2002)" (pp. 115–26), in *Chantal Akerman: Afterlives*, edited by Marion Schmid and Emma Wilson, Cambridge: Legenda.

Freud, Sigmund (1963), *Dora: An Analysis of a Case of Hysteria*, New York: Simon and Schuster.

Goethe, Johann Wolfgang von (2008), *Elective Affinities*, Oxford: Oxford University Press.

Golob, Sacha (2017), "Methodological Anxiety: Heidegger on Moods and Emotions" (pp. 253–71), in *Thinking about the Emotions: A Philosophical History*, Oxford: Oxford University Press.

Heberle, Helge and Monika Funke Stern (1982), "Das Feuer im Stern des Berges: Ein Gespräch mit Danièle Huillet von Helge Heberle und Monika Funke Stern," *Frauen und Film* 32: 4–12.

Hegel, G. W. F. (1986), *Enzyklopädie der philosophischen Wissenschaften III ("Encyclopedia III")*, Frankfurt am Main: Suhrkamp.

Hoberman, J. (1991), *Vulgar Modernism: Writing on Movies and Other Media*, Philadelphia: Temple University Press.

Hochschild, Arlie Russell (1983), *The Managed Heart: Commercialization of Human Feeling*, Berkeley: University of California Press.

Hopkins, Carmen Teeple (2017), "Mostly Work, Little Play: Social Reproduction, Migration, and Paid Domestic Work in Montreal" (pp. 131–47), in *Social Reproduction Theory: Remapping Class, Recentring Oppression*, edited by Tithi Bhattacharya, London: Pluto

Hornby, Louise (2017), *Still Modernism: Photography, Literature, and Film*, Oxford: Oxford University Press

Iversen, Margaret (2018), "World Without a Self: Edward Hopper and Chantal Akerman" (pp. 724–60), *Art History* 41: 4.

Jacobs, Steven (2012), "Semiotics of the Living Room: Domestic Interiors in Chantal Akerman's Cinema," (pp. 73-87) *Chantal Akerman: Too Far, Too Close*, Eke, Belgium: Ludion.

Kinder, Marsha (1989), "The Subversive Potential of the Pseudo-Iterative" (2 – 16), *Film Quarterly* 43: 2.

Kuhn, Annette (1994), *Women's Pictures: Feminism and Cinema*, Verso.

Lebow, Alisa (2003), "Memory Once Removed: Indirect Memory and Transitive Autobiography in Chantal Akerman's *D'Est*" (35-83) *Camera Obscura* 18: 1.

Loader, Jayne (1977), "Jeanne Dielman: Death in Installments," *Jump Cut* 16: 10-12.

Longfellow, Brenda (1989), "Love Letters to the Mother: The Work of Chantal Akerman" (73-90), *Canadian Journal of Political and Social Theory* 13: 1-2.

Lugones, Maria (1987), "Playfulness, 'World'-Travelling, and Loving Perception" (3-19), *Hypatia* 2: 2.

Lugones, Maria (1994), "Purity, Impurity, and Separation" (458-79), *Signs* 19: 2.

Mangolte, Babette (2019), *Selected Writings, 1998 – 2015,* Sternberg Press.

Margulies, Ivone (2003), "Echo and Voice in *Meetings with Anna*" (59-76), in *Identity and Memory: The Films of Chantal Akerman*, edited by Gwendolyn Audrey Foster, Carbondale: Southern Illinois University Press.

Margulies, Ivone (1996), *Nothing Happens: Chantal Akerman's Hyperrealist Everyday*, Durham: Duke University Press.

Margulies, Ivone (2016), "Elemental Akerman: Inside and Outside *No Home Movie*" (61-9), *Film Quarlerly* 70: 1.

Marso, Lori (2016), "Perverse Protests: Simone de Beauvoir on Pleasure and Danger, Resistance, and Female Violence in Film" (727-1018), *Signs* 41: 4.

Mayne, Judith (1990), *Woman at the Keyhole: Feminism and Women's Cinema*, Indiana University Press.

Mayne, Judith (2003), "Girl Talk: *Portrait of a Young Girl at the End of the 1960s in Brussels*" (150-61), in *Identity and Memory: The Films of Chantal Akerman*, edited by Gwendolyn Audrey Foster, Carbondale: Southern Illinois University Press.

McDonald, Tamar Jeffers (2007), *Romantic Comedy: Boy Meets Girl Meets Genre*, London: Wallflower.

Miller, Zara Joan (2020), "Repetition and Insistence in Akerman and Bausch," *Another Gaze* 4: 120-5.

Mulhall, Stephen (2015), *On Film*, Routledge.

Mulvey, Laura (1999), "Visual Pleasure and Narrative Cinema" (833-44), in *Film Theory and Criticism: Introductory Readings*, edited by Leo Braudy and Marshall Cohen, New York: Oxford University Press.

Murray, Ros (2016), "The Radical Politics of Possibility: Towards a Queer Existential Phenomenology through Chantal Akerman's Je tu il elle (1975)," *Feral Feminisms* 5: 44-56.

Murray, Ros (2019), "Revisiting Jeanne Dielman: Autour de Jeanne Dielman (2004), Woman Sitting After Killing (2001), and Akerman's 'cinéma de ressassement'," *Moving Image Review and Art Journal* 8(1–2): 54–66.

Myles, Eileen (2024), "inside 'i, you, he, she'" (49–52), in *Chantal Akerman, Traveling*, Brussels: Bozar-Centre for Fine Arts.

Okin, Susan (1989), *Justice, Gender, and the Family*, New York: Basic Books.

Ortega, Mariana (2016), *In-Between: Latina Feminist Phenomenology, Multiplicity, and the Self*, SUNY Press.

Pollock, Griselda (2010), "The Long Journey: Maternal Trauma, Tears and Kisses in a Work by Chantal Akerman," *Studies in the Maternal* 2: 1.

Proust, Marcel (1923), *The Prisoner*, translated by Carol Clark, Pengiun Books.

Pursley, Darlene (2005), "Moving in Time: Chantal Akerman's *Toute une nuit*" (1192–205), *MLN* 120: 5.

Rennebohm, Kate (2016), "La Ressasseuse: Chantal Akerman, 1950–2015," *Cinema Scope* 65: 6–9.

Rennebohm, Kate (2023), "Chantal Akerman and Stanley Cavell: Viewing in *La Captive* and Reviewing in Moral Perfection" (253–73), in *Movies with Stanley Cavell in Mind*, edited by David LaRocca, London: Bloomsbury.

Roberts, Adam (2019), "Blogging" (173–215) in *Chantal Akerman Retrospective Handbook*, edited by Joanna Hogg and Adam Roberts, London: A Nos Amours.

Roberts, Adam (2019), "'Like a Musical Piece': Akerman and Musicality" (127–38), in *Chantal Akerman: Afterlives*, edited by Marion Schmid and Emma Wilson, Cambridge: Legenda.

Rosenbaum, Jonathan (2016), "Place and Displacement," in *Chantal Akerman: Four Films*.

Rothfeld, Becca (2024), *All Things Are Too Small: Essays in Praise of Excess*, Metropolitan Books.

Rowley, Alison (2010), "Between Les Rendez-vous d'Anna and Demain on Déménage" (1–15), *Studies in the Maternal* 2: 1.

Schmid, Marion (2010), *Chantal Akerman*, Manchester: Manchester University Press.

Shaviro, Steven (2007), "Cliches of Identity: Chantal Akerman's Musicals" (11–17), *Quarterly Review of Film and Video* 24: 1.

Silverman, Kaja (2015), *The Miracle of Analogy: Or, The History of Photography, Part 1*, Stanford: Stanford University Press.

Sitney, Adams (2002), "Structural Film" (347–70), in *Visionary Film: The American Avant-Garde, 1943–2000*, Oxford University Press.

Skvirsky, Salome Aguilera (2020), *The Process Genre: Cinema and the Aesthetic of Labor*, Durham: Duke University Press.

Smallwood, Christine (2024), *La Captive*, Fireflies.

Sontag, Susan (2001), *Against Interpretation: And Other Essays*, Picador.

Taubin, Amy (2016), "Bordering on Documentary," in *Chantal Akerman: Four Films*.
Turim, Maureen (2003), "Personal pronouncements in *I...You...He...She*...and *Portrait of a Young Girl at the End of the 1960s in Brussels*" (9–26), in *Identity and Memory: The Films of Chantal Akerman*, edited by Gwendolyn Audrey Foster, Carbondale: Southern Illinois University Press.
Veltman, Andrea (2004), "The Sisyphean Torture of Housework: Simone de Beauvoir and the Inequitable Division of Domestic Work in Marriage" (121–43), *Hypatia* 19: 3.
Völcker, Tine Rahel (2020), *Chantal Akermans Verschwinden*, Leipzig: Spector.
Walsh, Maria (2019), "*News From Home* the Redux Version: Amodal Perception and 'la jouissance du voir'" (29–38), *Moving Image Review & Art Journal* 8: 1–2.
White, Jerry (2005), "Chantal Akerman's Revisionist Aesthetic" (47–68), in *Women and Experimental Filmmaking*, edited by Jean Petrolle and Virginia Wright Wexman, Urbana: University of Illinois Press.
White, Kenneth (2010), "Urban Unknown: Chantal Akerman in New York City" (365–78), *Screen* 51: 4.
White, Patricia (2008), "Lesbian Minor Cinema" (410–25), *Screen* 49: 4.
Wilson, Emma (2019), "Unknown Deaths in La Captive" (90–101), in *Chantal Akerman: Afterlives*, edited by Marion Schmid and Emma Wilson, Cambridge: Legenda.
Zambreno, Kate (2019), *Appendix Project: Talks and Essays*, Semiotext(e).
Zambreno, Kate (2020), *Drifts*, New York: Riverhead.

# INDEX

abstraction   25, 57, 95
acoustics   40, 50–1, 158, 193 n.14
acting   93, 124, 140, *see also* deconstruction; non-naturalism
Ahmed, Sarah   157, 193 n.10
Akerman, Chantal
   *Autoportrait en Cinéaste*   19 n.5, 21 n.39, 60 n.8, 64 n.65, 64 n.71
   *Autour de Jeanne Dielman*   94, 102, 124, 127
   biography   1–7
   *Blow Up My Town*   67–71, 81–6, 100, 104 n.7
   *A Couch in New York*   118, 136–42, 151 n.53, 151 n.60
   *D'Est*   24, 43–8
   *The Eighties*   123–9, 149 n.37
   *Family Business*   4, 151 n.63
   *A Family in Brussels*   104 n.10
   filmmaking style   16, 35, 93, 139
   *From the Other Side*   48–59, 65 n.76
   *Golden Eighties*   117–18, 123–5, 128–36, 141
   *Hotel Monterey*   1, 24, 36–9, 44, 56, 90
   *I'm Hungry, I'm Cold*   154, 175–8, 192 n.6
   *Jeanne Dielman 23, quai du Commerce 1080 Bruxelles*   3, 10, 67–103
   *Je Tu Il Elle*   154–60, 162–7, 190, 194 n.19, 194 n.23, 195 n.3, 198 n.73, 198 n.75, 199 n.83
   *Là-Bas*   59 n.1, 65 n.81
   *La Captive*   154, 182–92
   *La Chambre*   6, 13–14
   *L'Enfant aimé ou je joue à être une femme mariée*   193 n.14
   *Letters Home*   193 n.14
   *Man with a Suitcase*   70
   *Meetings with Anna*   154, 151 n.63, 167–75, 192 n.6, 198 n.74
   *My Mother Laughs*   3, 11, 107 n.52
   *News from Home*   24, 36, 39–43
   *Night and Day*   197 n.63
   *No Home Movie*   53–9
   *Portrait of a Young Girl at the End of the 60s in Brussels*   154, 176, 178–82, 197 n.68, 198 n.74
   reception   3–4, 6, 62 n.49, 108 n.57, 167–8, 195 n.38, 198 n.79
   *Sud*   59 n.1, 59 n.7, 65 n.76
Akerman, Natalia (Nelly)   1, 53–9, 96, 147 n.5, *see also No Home Movie*
Akerman, Sylviane   54
*The Albertine Workout* (Carson)   191
alienation   28, 43, 60 n.14, 63 n.54, 90, 92, 108 n.67, 119
"All the Boys and Girls of Their Age,"   178
Almeida, Gabriela   151 n.6
ambivalence   109 n.69, 110 n.84, 117, 196 n.47

## INDEX

*Annie Hall* (dir. Woody Allen)   151 n.53
Anzaldúa, Gloria   29, 31, 34, 40, 51
artificiality   131–2, 149 n.6
Atherton, Claire   2, 5, 13, 64 n.63
attention
 of Anna   171–2, 175
 of audience   39, 91, 115, 172
 of Chantal Akerman   26, 36, 44, 50, 70
 of *Jeanne Dielman*   98–101
Auschwitz   1, 58, 107 n.52, *see also* Holocaust
auteur   5
*Autoportrait en Cinéaste* (Akerman)   19 n.5, 21 n.39, 60 n.8, 64 n.65, 64 n.71
*Autour de Jeanne Dielman* (dir. Frey)   94, 102, 124, 127

Barthes, Roland   147 n.4
Bausch, Pina   107 n.50, 109 n.69
being-at-home   11, 25–30, 57
Benjamin, Walter   12, 64 n.65
Bergstrom, Janet   148 n.17, 148 n.22
Berlant, Lauren   115–16, 122
*Bilderverbot*   2
Binoche, Juliette   138, 143
Blanchot, Maurice   12
*Blow Up My Town* (dir. Akerman)   67–71, 81–6, 100, 104 n.7
bodies   25, 44, 47–50, 59 n.1, 88, 155, 162, 193 n.15
 cinema of   155
Borden, Lizzie   108 n.54
borderlands   31–2, 51
Brown, James   182
Brussels   1, 20 n.22, 35, 39, 40, 47, 53, 55, 58, 104 n.10, 110 n.77, 114, 123, 127, 147 n.1, 154, 168, 176, 178

Butler, Judith   149 n.38
Butler, Kristine   62 n.40

*Cahiers du Cinema*   148 n.8
Camus, Albert   105 n.15
captivity   11, 191–2
Carson, Anne   160–5, 190–1
Cavell, Stanley   8, 27–8, 93, 108 n.55, 109 n.72, 118–19, 146
Chamarette, Jenny   192 n.5, 194 n.19
class   76–8, 105 n.27, 106 n.30
Clément, Aurore   188, 195 n.41, 195 n.43, 196 n.44
comedy of remarriage   146–7, *see also* romantic comedy
consciousness   9, 28, 30, 60 n.14, 95, 108 n.67
 consciousness-raising   77, 101, 106 n.29
Conway, Kelley   150 n.50, 177, 193 n.15, 195–6 n.43, 197 n.65, 200 n.99
Corpas, Irene Valle   59 n.5, 62 n.45, 93, 107 n.49
*A Couch in New York* (dir. Akerman)   118, 136–42, 151 n.53, 151 n.60

Davis, Angela   78
de Beauvoir, Simone   72–5, 78–9, 86, 105 n.24
Debré, Constance   160, 174, 194 n.23
deconstruction   125, 149 n.37
Decorte, Jan   4
de Kuyper, Eric   184
Deleuze, Gilles   12, 155, 192 n.6
Demy, Jacques   132, 150 n.47
desire
 as bittersweet   160–1, 166

erotic 154–5, 159, 160, 190
obsessive 183–4, 199 n.92
queer 154, 157, 160, 176, 193 n.17
*D'Est* (dir. Akerman) 24, 43–8
Despentes, Virginie 104 n.4
dialogue 12, 93, 136, 139
difference 10, 25, 34, 142, 175
documentary
 films 6, 33, 36, 40, 49, 53, 59 n.7, 65 n.81, 109 n.69
 "making-of" 94–6, 123–4
 practice 26–8, 60 n.8
domesticity 1, 68, 78, 81–6, 92, 96, 106 n.33, 122, 145, 196 n.52
Dreyfus, Hubert 109 n.68
dualisms 10–11, 13, 24, *see also* oppositions
Duras, Marguerite 108 n.55
duration 14–15, 18, 43, 86, 107 n.51
Dyer, Richard 132, 150 n.49

Edelman, Lee 193
Ehrenburg, Sidonie 2
*The Eighties* (dir. Akerman) 123–9, 149 n.37
Elpidorou, Andreas 60 n.18, 60 n.19
emotions 115, 117, 133, 145, *see also feeling rules*
Ephron, Nora 137
*Eros the Bittersweet* (Carson) 160–5, 190
eternal recurrence 79, 135, 146
experimental film 13, 35, 117, 124, 151 n.53
exploitation 77–8, 80–1

*Family Business* (dir. Akerman) 4, 151 n.63
*A Family in Brussels* (Akerman) 104 n.10
fantasy 28, 119, 128, 134, 198 n.69
father (Jacques Akerman) 1, 4, 46, 139
Federici, Silvia 76–81, 87, 101, 106 n.29
Feeling rules 116–17, 120, 126, *see also emotions*
Felski, Rita 110 n.84
female friendship 178, 180, 197 n.65
feminism 6, 29–31, 68–70, 76–9, 87–8, 91, 106 n.28, 106 n.36, 110 n.84, 110 n.85, 194 n.30
Fenz, Robert 65 n.75
Fischer, Lucy 149 n.29, 149 n.36
Flitterman-Lewis, Sandy 19 n.6, 59 n.2
Forrester, Katrina 106 n.28
Foster, Gwendolyn 124, 149 n.27, 149 n.37, 149 n.38, 150 n.45
Fowler, Catherine 147, 150 n.42, 150 n.43, 150 n.47, 150 no.48
Fox, Albertine 65 n.75, 65 n.77
freedom 11, 63 n.54, 74, 92, 117, 167–8, 191–2, 197 n.56
Freeman, Lauren 60 n.19
Freud, Sigmund 172
Frey, Sami 109
*From the Other Side* (dir. Akerman) 48–59, 65 n.76

gender 105 n.21, 126, 157, 166, 177, 193 n.9, 195 n.36
genre 117–19, 122, 136–40
Godard, Jean-Luc 2, 85, 155, 167–9, 195 n.39
Goethe, Johann Wolfgang 45

*Golden Eighties* (dir. Akerman) 117–18, 123–5, 128–36, 141
Golob, Sacha 60 n.19

habit 9
Hadland, Gracie 194 n.23
Heberle, Helge 108 n.64
Hegel, G. W. F. 9–12
Heidegger, Martin 28–32, 56
Hitchcock, Alfred 14, 88, 183, 186, 198 n.79
Hoberman, J. 125, 127, 149 n.39
Hochschild, Arlie 116–17
Hoens, Dominiek 119, 148 n.21
Hollywood 88, 108 n.59, 132
Holocaust 58, 133, 150 n.50, 171, *see also* Auschwitz
home, *see also* being-at-home
 not being at 29–30, 57
 in *News from Home* 39–40, 43
 in *No Home Movie* 53–9
 in Latina feminist philosophy 32–5
Hopkins, Carmen Teeple 106 n.33
Hopper, Edward 38, 63 n.54
Hornby, Louise 188, 199 n.85
*Hotel Monterey* (dir. Akerman) 1, 24, 36–9, 44, 56, 90
housework
 in *Blow Up My Town* 68–72, 81–3
 in *A Couch in New York* 140
 feminist criticisms 69–70, 72–81, 105 n.15, 105 n.22, 106 n.28, 106 n.30, 106 n.34, 106 n.36
 in *Jeanne Dielman* 68–72, 86–7, 89–94, 97–8, 100–1, 108 n.54
Hurt, William 138, 143
hyperrealism 91

*I'm Hungry, I'm Cold* (dir. Akerman) 154, 175–8, 192 n.6
identity 6, 10, 24, 33–4, 59 n.2, 63 n.55, 104 n.8, 160, 165, 174, 194 n.22
images 17, 90, 114, 117
immanence 73–5, 92, 98, *see also* transcendence
Indiana, Gary 102–3, 123, 194 n.29
interiority 15–16, 18, 111 n.88, 155, 182, 190
Irigaray, Luce 12
Israel 53, 65 n.81, 66 n.86
Iversen, Margaret 43, 61 n.36, 63 n.54

Jacobs, Steven 21 n.36
*Jazz Singer* (dir. Crosland) 150 n.46
*Jeanne Dielman 23, quai du Commerce 1080 Bruxelles* (dir. Akerman) 3–4, 7–10, 67–103, 114, *Je Tu Il Elle* (dir. Akerman) 154–60, 162–7, 190, 194 n.19, 194 n.23, 195 n.3, 198 n.73, 198 n.75, 199 n.83
169, 172, 192 n.5, 196 n.52
Jewish 1, 6, 20 n.25, 24, 59 n.2, 96, 128, 150 n.46
Joyce, James 179

Kant, Immanuel 146
Kierkegaard, Soren 146, 178
Kinder, Marsha 114, 147 n.7
knowledge of others 16, 58, 102–4, 187, 199 n.89, 199 n.92, *see also* unknowability
Kuhn, Annette 108 n.60

*L'Amore Perdonera* (Lorenzi) 120
*Là-Bas* (dir. Akerman) 59 n.1, 65 n.81

Lacan, Jacques   12, 141
*La Captive* (dir. Akerman)   154, 182–92
*La Chambre* (dir. Akerman)   6, 13–14
*La Region Centrale* (dir. Snow)   2
Lebow, Alisa   64 n.68, 65 n.83
*L'Enfant aimé ou je joue à être une femme mariée* (dir. Akerman)   193 n.14
lesbian   6, 34, 72, 108 n.67, 156–7, 160–1, 164, 178, 188, 190, 194 n.30, 196 n.52, 197 n.67, 197 n.68, 198 n.74, 200 n.94, 200 n.96
*Letters Home* (dir. Akerman)   193 n.14
Levinas, Emmanuel   12, 63 n.58
liminal
   film   117
   spaces   31, 38, 168
literary adaptations   182, 198 n.76
loneliness   8, 119
Longfellow, Brenda   108 n.67, 155–9
Lopatin, Amanda   196 n.52
love
   falling in   138, 142, 145, 176
   romantic   114–16, 119, 134, 145–6, 157, 160
*Love Me Tender* (Debré)   174, 194 n.23
Lubitsch, Ernst   137, 140
Lugones, Maria   29, 32–5, 40, 50, 60 n.21, 61 n.26, 61 n.31, 62 n.37

male gaze   87, 89, 195 n.32, *see also* Laura Mulvey
Mangolte, Babette   2, 5–6, 20 n.22, 35–6, 43, 51, 59 n.1, 96
*Man with a Suitcase* (dir. Akerman)   70

Margulies, Ivone   3, 62 n.47, 65 n.84, 66 n.86, 66 n.92, 91, 104 n.5, 104 n.8, 109 n.74, 114, 129, 147 n.2, 147 n.7, 148 n.23, 149 n.31, 149 n.35, 194 n.22, 195 n.34, 195 n.35, 195 n.37, 196 n.45, 196 n.47, 197 n.56, 197 n.60
marriage   75, 105 n.21, 108 n.56, 115–16, 122, 133–4, 144–7
Marso, Lori   108 n.56
Martin, Adrian   151 n.62, 152 n.66
Marx, Karl   21 n.36
Maslin, Janet   137, 172
Mayne, Judith   157, 180, 193 n.9, 194 n.31, 195 n.33, 195 n.36, 197 n.68, 198 n.69
McDonald, Tamar Jeffers   136
mechanism   74, 93
*Meetings with Anna* (dir. Akerman)   151 n.63, 154, 167–75, 192 n.6, 198 n.74
Mexico   49–52
Miller, Zara Joan   86, 109 n.69
minimalism   4, 38–9, 56, 195 n.34
mood   30, 63 n.54, 65 n.84, 115, 124
mothers, *see also* Golden Eighties; The Eighties
   in *A Couch in New York*   140–1
   in *La Captive*   198 n.80
   in *News from Home* (*see News from Home*)
   in *No Home Movie* (*see No Home Movie*)
   in philosophy   33–5, 75, 80, 101, *see also* Akerman, Natalia (Nelly)
Mulvey, Laura   87–8, 108 n.59
Murray, Ros   111 n.86, 193 n.17
musicals   4, 118, 123–36
Myles, Eileen   158

*My Mother Laughs* (Akerman)   3, 11, 107 n.52
mystery   111 n.88, 115, 143, 145

Narboni, Jean   193
*News from Home* (dir. Akerman)   24, 36, 39–43
New York   2–4, 6, 9, 14, 20 n.25, 23, 35–41, 56, 62 n.43, 63 n.53, 136–42, 151 n.53, 151 n.60, 154, 159
Nietzsche, Friedrich   79
*Night and Day* (dir. Akerman)   197 n.63
*No Home Movie* (dir. Akerman)   53–9
non-naturalism   93, 140
Nunonda, Erin   178

Okin, Susan   105 n.21
*Oklahoma* (dir. Zinneman)   132
oppositions   24, 71, 122, 155
Ortega, Mariana   29, 31–2, 60 n.21, 61 n.25, 61 n.26, 61 n.31

Païni, Dominik   151 n.57
passion   120, 122, 134, 145, 147 n.7, 148 n.23, 180
perception   8, 32, 61 n.31, 61 n.32, 64 n.63, 125, 144, 162
performance   117, 126, 149 n.35, 164
performativity   149 n.38
philosophy   7, 12, 21, 29, 146, 192
Piaf, Edith   169
*Pierrot le Fou* (dir. Godard)   2, 85, 155
Plato   150 n.44
*Playboy* (Debré)   160
pleasure
    aesthetic   17

of female friendship   178, 180, 197 n.65
in *Jeanne Dielman*   92, 95, 97, 98, 101, 108–9 n.67, 110 n.79
visual   87–8, 149 n.35
of watching   2, 142, 182
*Portrait of a Young Girl at the End of the 60s in Brussels* (dir. Akerman)   154, 176, 178–82, 197 n.68, 198 n.74
*Portrait of the Artist as a Young Man* (Joyce)   179
potatoes   9, 86–7, 90, 92, 99, 104, 107 n.51, 107 n.5
privacy   16–17, 38, 54, 58, 103, 183
"The Prisoner" (Proust)   182, 191–2
Proust, Marcel   16, 182, 190–2, 198 n.78

Rainer, Yvonne   104 n.8
Ravez, Agnes   109 n.74
Rennebohm, Kate   66 n.88, 107 n.46, 187, 199 n.91, 200 n.93
*Revolution Point Zero* (Federici)   80–81, 106 n.29
Roberts, Adam   110 n.81, 115, 148 n.9, 149 n.40
romantic comedy   118, 136–8
Rosenbaum, Jonathan   51, 60 n.14, 65 n.74, 65 n.76, 65 n.79, 65 n.80
Rothfeld, Becca   194 n.28
Rowley, Alison   193 n.17
Rubin, Nathan   151 n.64

Schmid, Marion   21 n.34, 44, 62 n.43, 63 n.59, 64 n.61, 64 n.65, 64 n.69, 83, 103 n.2, 107 n.47, 147 n.4, 162, 193 n.8, 194 n.20, 195 n.32, 198 n.71, 198 n.73, 199 n.92, 200 n.98

*The Second Sex* (de Beauvoir)   72–5, 78–9, 86
secret   1, 103, 111 n.88, 172–3, 187, 196 n.49
Sellars, Wilfrid   21 n.32
sex
   in *I'm Hungry, I'm Cold*   177–8
   in *Jeanne Dielman*   3, 90, 92, 97, 108 n.54
   in *Je Tu Il Elle*   156–7, 162–5, 193 n.15, 193 n.17, 194 n.40
   in *La Captive*   186, 189
   in *Portrait of a Young Girl*   179
Seyrig, Delphine   5, 90–1, 94–5, 102–3, 109 n.74, 127, 195 n.41, 195 n.43
Shaviro, Steven   150 n.44, 150 n.47, 150 n.51
*The Shop Around the Corner* (dir. Lubitsch)   137, 140
*Sight and Sound*   4, 62 n.49, 108 n.57, 198 n.79
Silverman, Kaja   185, 199 n.83, 199 n.84, 199 n.86, 199 n.89
Singer, Isaac Bashevis   20 n.15, 195 n.39
*Singing in the Rain* (dir. Kelly and Donen)   132
Singularity   5, 69, 115, 147 n.7, 148 n.23, 152 n.68
Sisyphus   72, 105 n.15
Sitney, P. Adams   35, 61 n.35
Skvirsky, Salomé Aguilera   20–1 n.29, 94, 107 n.41, 109 n.73, 110 n.80
*Sleepless in Seattle* (dir. Ephron)   137
Smallwood, Christine   111 n.88, 196 n.49, 197 n.61, 198 n.77, 199 n.92, 200 n.103
Snow, Michael   2, 13–14

Sontag, Susan   17, 150 n.45
structural film   35, 61 n.35
subjectivity   43, 155–6, 165
*Sud* (dir. Akerman)   59 n.1, 59 n.7, 65 n.76

Taubin, Amy   60 n.16, 103 n.1
teleology   157, 177
thinking
   Akerman   13, 66 n.87
   in *Jeanne Dielman*   93, 95, 98, 102
*Toute une nuit* (dir. Akerman)   113–15, 117–22
transcendence   73–4, 105 n.20, *see also* immanence
trauma   16, 51, 63 n.55, 97, 100
triangulation   161–4, 173, 175–7, 184, 197 n.63, *see also* desire
Turim, Maureen   194 n.30, 195 n.35, 198 n.75

*Umbrellas of Cherbourg* (dir. Demy)   132, 150 n.47
United States of America   32, 48–9, 52, 148 n.25
unknowability   16, 58, 188
unsocial sociability   146

van der Lint, Roos   104 n.7
Veltman, Andrea   105 n.22
Vermeer, Johannes   38
*Vertigo* (dir. Hitchcock)   88, 183, 198 n.79
*A Very Easy Death* (de Beauvoir)   75, 105 n.24
violence   32, 72, 88
Vöckler, Tine Rahel   19 n.2
voyeurism   88–9, 194 n.29
vulnerability   48, 122

Wages For Housework   76–9, 89,
    106 n.28
White, Jerry   63 n.55, 149 n.29,
    149 n.32, 151 n.62
White, Patricia   21 n.30, 197 n.67,
    198 n.74
White, Stephen   151 n.57
Wieder-Atherton, Sonia
    5

Wilson, Emma   199 n.87, 199 n.92,
    200 n.97
Woolf, Virginia   81, 192 n.6
*Working Girls* (dir. Borden)   108 n.54
world-travel   29, 32–5, 40, 50, 60
    n.21, 61 n.26, 61 n.31, 62 n.37

Zambreno, Kate   20 n.22, 38, 54,
    63 n.51